I0796736

MANIFEST DESTINY

ALSO BY PELUMI OLATINPO

Poeta: Sonetas and Sonnets

MANIFEST DESTINY

PELUMI OLATINPO

TogetherInWitness

Published by TogetherInWitness
Sheridan, WY 82801
www.TogetherInWitness.org
Instagram: @togetherinwitness
hello@togetherinwitness.org

ISBN (Hardcover): 979-8-9906763-9-8
ISBN (eBook): 979-8-9906763-8-1
Library of Congress Control Number: 2025939472

Published in the United States of America

Illustrations and typesetting by Tanja Dabic
Book design by Pelumi Olatinpo

1 3 5 7 9 10 8 6 4 2

First Edition

INVOCATION

I do not come to you alone. Naked. Without guests.
I do not come to you alone. Wounded. Without songs.
Without the calabash of fire burning in my chest.
Without the voices of the ancestors sitting in my lungs.
I do not come to you, dear friend. Without fear.
Afraid the living. Proud. Errors of the dead. Loudly wear.

On the Soneta

MANIFEST DESTINY is the continuation of my life's work, which began with my earlier creation, *Poeta*, where I introduced a new poetic form: the **soneta**.

The soneta is a six-line poem with no more than ten words per line, and a fixed rhyme scheme of poet choice (for example: AAAAAA, AAABBB, ABCABC, among others). It traces its roots from the traditional English sonnet (*sonetto* in Italian, which means 'little song') of fourteen lines; the musical form sonata, which is derived from Latin *sonare*, that is, 'to sound;' and the aural power of West African oral traditions. As a result of this eclectic and rhapsodic heritage, the soneta possesses a musical allure that's almost inescapable, impossible to resist—particularly when read aloud. It immerses the reader in what I love to call a "blood and bones" experience.

The soneta, at its core, is a highly compressed poem. It seeks to pack the entirety of a mansion in a single room while showcasing the glamor of artful order and power of focused expression. The soneta never sacrifices precision for depth, concision for complexity, accessibility for profundity.

Like the English sonnet with three core rules (lines, rhymes, meter), the soneta's rules (lines, rhymes, words) create an operating theater where the poet is a surgeon working feverishly to bring to life what otherwise would lie lifeless, silenced, forgotten in the hallways and waiting rooms of the human condition.

I hope this work, building on the foundation of *Poeta*, transforms you; that you become all you've ever imagined to be and could be—even then, unimaginably more. I hope it lights something in you that makes you sing the song your soul was always meant to sing.

A Note to Readers:
This work includes explanatory endnotes at the end of each Book (there are four in total, following a narrative arc). These provide historical and literary insights for those interested in deeper context. Feel free to engage with them as you read, or explore them after finishing each Book—whichever best suits your experience. These notes are not an exhaustive treatise of all the possible inspirations and interpretations of the sonetas but are breadcrumbs to help guide you home.

MANIFEST DESTINY was composed between 2024 and early 2025. Some sonetas address events that were still unfolding during final manuscript preparation, particularly the Israel-Hamas conflict (October 2023-March 2025). Endnotes reflect data available as of March 2025.

Contents

[8] Speak up for those who cannot speak for themselves;
ensure justice for those being crushed.
[9] Yes, speak up for the poor and helpless,
and see that they get justice.

Proverbs 31 (NLT)

[3] Defend the weak and the orphans;
defend the rights of the poor and suffering.
[4] Save the weak and helpless;
free them from the power of the wicked.

Psalm 82 (NCV)

MANIFEST DESTINY

BOOK I:

FIRST LIGHT

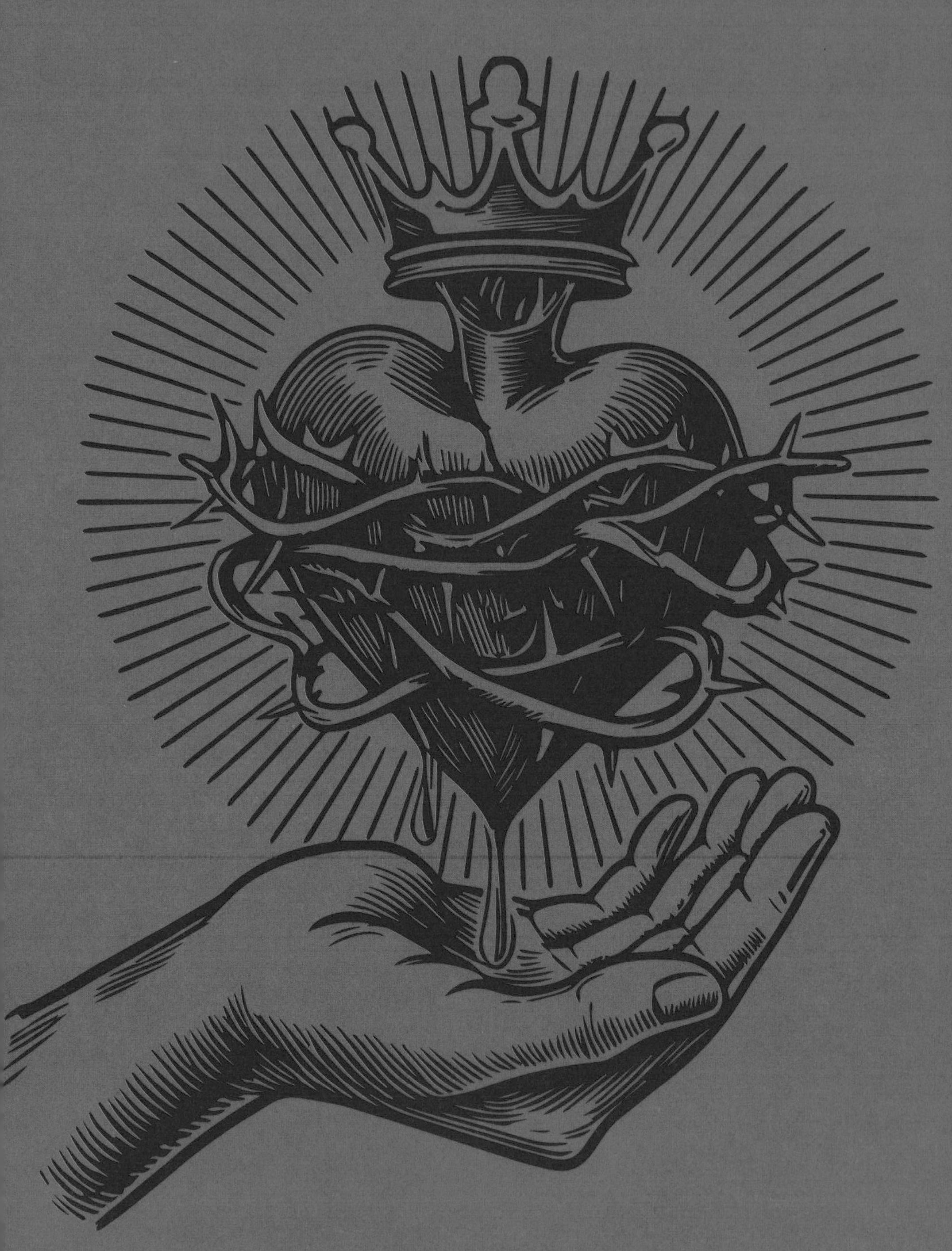

Songs of Love

(Sonetas 247-257)

SONETA 247

My love, let me love you with all the love
Your majesty requires. Open your mouth and let me
Slow-feed you the sweetness of love, like dew from above,
Like were honey, stolen from God's sugary tree.
Open the doors of your chest, let me kiss your heart,
Dangle your legs, let me caress your insides, like art.

SONETA 248

Like sweet morning dew, I took one look at you
And knew—you were too true not to pursue,
Too good not to push through—all rules and queues—
To view your truth, with every brew, and morning news.
So I gave my life, to testify—all I need
Is ever you; I'd gladly bleed, to see you succeed.

SONETA 249

They say Time is money, but somehow, you and I
Never got to be rich. It always seemed we worked
Some strange hours, very long hours, caught a red-eye
Just to strike it BIG. I hustled while you talked,
You bustled while I sulked. We never could grow together,
So borrowed to stay together, till we were broke forever.

SONETA 250

These fine lines which brightly shine
Are finely lined by the beauty of thy divine kind.
For my mind—blessed of thee and fully thine—
Nightly write lines sensuous as June, wherein thou art enshrined,
And forever bound. Thus, poets to be, looking for light,
In these lines shall brightness find, in your sunshine delight.

SONETA 251

I would have loved you more, if more
Were a beast, wild and unchained, fine and untamed,
Which no king had ever reined, nor claimed for store.
If more were a duty, sure as prophecy, pained
And unrestrained, to dig a well at gate of hell.
Would have ridden this beast, fetched you water, from hell.

SONETA 252

Haunt me like sin. Cut me like teeth.
Scrape me down like steel. Till no seasons I see,
No freedom I breathe, but in your burrow I writhe,
If I ever your beauty should leave, for she,
Born with wreath, rich like queen of ancient Kush—
For your poverty, sweet like peach, against heaven will push.

SONETA 253

I have fought at love, and fallen, in love,
Here, on these battle-wearied slopes, lodged between the corpses of
Someone's bloodied sons, and some weathered wagon, used for ferrying
Souls of broken hopes, felled in love's fiery forging,
To flowerless, unremarkable graves. Whatsoever shall be said of me?
That I fought so bravely like thunder, torn asunder. Completely.

SONETA 254

Shall I give you what your will, will not take?
Force upon your tender heart a solemn love,
Pure and true, yet, so frail, mine could break?
Yes, to your will have I sworn, like a dove
Faithful till death; must will then against will hate?
Mine your pleasure to seek, yours, mine to subjugate?

SONETA 255

How shall I bid thee another tongue to speak
When within the edifice of thy mouth
A foreign tongue now resides, foreign to me,
But not to thee—thou wert pledged this very week.
Yet do I sense in thee a desire to shout,
Shout my name, as duty wars against love, within thee.

SONETA 256

Renounce his name on love's sacred account.
No more his name bear than you would a moment
Endure, and be injured, by sorrow's hateful dagger.
Happily my name pronounce, which surmounts all ill in amount,
Take that foulest part of me, in covenant,—bountiful bestowment,
For in claiming my name, you crown king a beggar.

SONETA 257

Whisper the secret of our love in mine ear.
Touch this untouched ear with the sweet softness
Of your lips. Flood my mouth with waters like myrrh;
Dip me in your breasts' fountain, swallow me like darkness.
Many mighty kings, many thirsty paupers have sought this lotion,
Fought to drink this potion. When you are love's ocean.

Hidden Waters

(Sonetas 258-268)

SONETA 258

Àṣàkẹ́, what is childhood? The years I didn't know
I was alive? Didn't know beaded masquerades danced with whips,
Didn't know how fast, and strange, time crawls, and stalls?
What is childhood? Can someone recall my pinky toe,
Why it healed so scarred and black? Did I trip
Upon the asphalt, cut myself into adulthood, imagined the fall?

SONETA 259

Like nuns in a nunnery, sworn to bouts of silence,
So are the days my eyes cling to your grace
But forbidden to speak. For in quietus, quietness
Of mouth yet loudness of mind, I hear your gaze
Call to me, as I to you,—but this vow
That clothes our lips, gladness and joy coldly disallow.

SONETA 260

There's a trapdoor beneath the rug in my room,
Squeaky and steely; so when I count sheep
That wouldn't sleep, feel fountain deep that wouldn't seal,
I wonder what tired creature moves and looms,
Sits and fumes, within the dark keep, and sometimes weep.
The night glows with ghosts, what ghouls will they unseal?

SONETA 261

I want to be free. I want to succeed.
Flee this dungeon of hate. Forgive myself for my deed.
Bleed these demons in my heart; tell 'em—*I'm freed!*
I want to stampede from this prison I'm keyed.
Like Jonah in the deep, sightless, surrounded by seaweed,
All alone in my guilt. Forsaken. Mercy flees, won't concede.

SONETA 262

Rachel weeps for a fee, so she can feed
Her kids. Soggy lashes, long, dark, and heavy
As Death himself, greet flowery caskets, every Saturday, as agreed.
She soon must hurry along, scurry home, before Judy,
The babysitter, charges another hour, and her landlord,
Shouts again, for rent two-months past due, she can't afford.

SONETA 263

Nothing about pain frightens me so I can cry,
Till I die. Nothing about joy jolts me
So I can laugh—till I fly. Nothing about life
Scares me, caresses me, cheers me, tears me,
That I sigh, wonder why, I'm alive and never high,
Nor ever low. Nothing. So I just wait … for afterlife.

SONETA 264

When you're a ghetto chef, you master the art
Of cooking crack, Talib once said. You cook
Not because you are a crook, or hooked
On some summertime high, eager to shoot off, like dart—
But master the art like crack were your schoolbook.
In the ghetto, life's the lighter, crack is your checkbook.

SONETA 265

I was born an inmate. Cell Block South Shore.
South Side, Chicago. Inmate Number 280904.
Sentenced at birth. Christened by Death. Felonies my cellmates.
Mama died in childbirth. Brother in gunfight. Death Row inmates.
Across blocks, violence plays like lullabies. Pavements stained like raspberries.
Warden says I'm animal. Withholds libraries. Promotes penitentiaries. Cemeteries.

SONETA 266

In the age of Adderall
We are all on a spectrum: *Judith, you're running*
Too fast! Jacob, slow down! You can never sit down!
Prisoners of science, surrendered to data, drugged to a crawl,
To keep from fleeing the ward. Paul once went plunging
Into river of toys; now, just stares, like a clown.

SONETA 267

I woke up this morning to sounds of clapping waters,
Chanting rivers, begging Freedom to be brave—from the sunny
Hills of Appalachia, to concrete jungles of Cascadia. Smolders, embers
Of Liberty, grasping for air,—from the bluegrass of Kentucky
To the blueberry farms of New Hampshire. I woke up
This morning, to swallows dying, crying—across the mountaintop.

SONETA 268

The demons amongst us we know, so we baffle not
At the fangs of their vitriol. The fence-sitters we know
Too well, so we sorrow not that they are naught.
But our friends have we not known, family like foe,
Though together we have bathed, together we have laughed,—
In that hour of truth... friends cowered like lifeless raft.

Rising Voice

(Sonetas 269-282)

SONETA 269

We were eight years in power, despite the color
Of our brother. We were eight years in power
Despite the assault of the birther proclaiming: *American, he's not.*
Since nobody questioned his rot, told him to stop. Fought.
He became a god, elected their thought—Racist or not.
We were eight years in power. Affordable Care we brought.

SONETA 270

Whitelash for every trespass. White lies for every Black rise.
With every climb, a constant sign: *Colored, Go No Farther!*
But we are a people on a journey—From Stagville
To Parrish Street, Colfax to Greenwood, Ocoee to Oval,—eyes
On the prize. No matter the trumpery of the birther,
We shall not be moved. We've sighted Canaan. Survived Charlottesville.

SONETA 271

Freedom of speech ain't never been free for me.
Ain't never been rich to buy speech. No, not ever.
Never bought a pound of speech to drink with tea
Like the rich man that sleeps at Ritz. No, not ever.
They say we Citizens United, but when they speak,
They crush my speech. Moneybags so loud drowns my shriek.

SONETA 272

I cain't never be woke. 'Cause to be woke
Provokes master. Master says we folk been free:
From Louisiana to Indiana—strange fruit on oak tree
No more. So when he knee my throat an' choke;
Cloaks my vote to keep control; freedom revoke
With them laws like strokes;—he'd rather I ain't spoke.

SONETA 273

The meek shall inherit the earth was not spoken
Of the weak, the bleak, the scared, but the freak,
The weird, the feared, who seek not the token
From master's table, but resist the antics of the critic
With gentle mystique—withstand Fortune's fangs with valiant defiance.
The meek shall inherit the earth was spoken of lions.

SONETA 274

Six Triple Eight. Black Doves in Hitler's war,
Soaring to defend the frontline wall: *no mail, low morale.*
Charity for heart, defiant in spite the vermin of Corps,
Adam's Eve proved what Adam's wit could not at all.
Blessed are the peacemakers—Black Doves. They shall be called:
Daughters of God, Repairers of breach, Light of the world.

SONETA 275

We fought at Appomattox. Braved with blood the guns
Of those who'd keep us enslaved. We were burned
At Fort Pillow, nailed to logs, dismembered, smote our sons.
Yet have we not asked Stars and Stripes what's unearned,
But daily fight to rise to Generals, Admirals—not servicemen
Enlisted to carry orders, segregated and subjugated, though we're countrymen.

SONETA 276

To the rejected, the dejected, scum of the earth,
Abused and confused by views du jour;
Disrespected and convicted by the scepter of wealth,
Marooned upon the island of life, consumed by the pressure
To survive; to myself, and all I would never be,—
Thine is the kingdom, the power, and the glory, eventually.

SONETA 277

Right to be free. Freedom to be right.
The anthem of every heart. The pining of every wight.
Liberty pangs within me, shackled by treachery, famished of Equity,
Bangs upon every door, slams upon every wall, of bigotry—
Calls America to be America! *Fulfill the letter of your charter.*
For all lives cannot matter, while many lives are fodder.

SONETA 278

We want to move on, but you won't let us.
What more do you want? Gave you your Black president,
Made you your Black holiday, still, you won't let us ...
Move on. Gave you, even, a lady justice—without precedent;
Still, you hound our feet, like a dog without leash—
Shouting you can't breathe, *can't breathe*, like a choking fish.

SONETA 279

What is progress? Can't dig a knife ten inches
Deep in my belly, pull out an inch, tell me—
It's progress! Can't loosen your knot that lynches
My black body, feet thrashing—thirty feet off the tree,
Tell me—*It's progress*. Can't steal two hundred forty-six years,
Forty acres, mule, refuse **fourfold**, tell me—*You're free! Cheers.*

SONETA 280

Has pain found an expiration date—a time I can
No more mourn for what was robbed, what was lost,
What was torn from the arms of love, dashed
Against the rocks of bondage. No one tells the man
Whose forebears burned in Hitler's oven: *forgive, forget, you must!*
Yet I, cruelly crushed, bleeding, quiet must be, newly gashed.

SONETA 281

They told me—*Hush! Toe the line. Be quiet.*
Know your place, don't disgrace your race!
This has got nothing to do with you;
Gotta save the Jews, so don't cause a riot.
They drop bombs like rain on Gaza—erase her face
Forever. No, not in my name. I won't let you!

SONETA 282

The spirit of the Lord God is upon me
For He has given me the tongue of the learned
To speak a word in season to him that's weary
Ferry the load of him that's heavy, stormed, and soulburned.
I've not hidden my face from shame, body from tormentors,
For I know His counsel is forever,—against all persecutors.

Endnotes for BOOK I: FIRST LIGHT

Songs of Love (Sonetas 247-257)

Soneta 247: "My love, let me love you with all the love..."

Like were honey, stolen from God's sugary tree: Draws directly from the Tree of Life in Genesis 2-3 and Revelation 22:2, which bears "twelve manner of fruits" and leaves "for the healing of the nations." The poem transforms divine sustenance into romantic metaphor, elevating human love to sacred significance.

Sonetas 254-256:

These interconnected sonetas explore forbidden love and competing loyalties. The sequence presents a narrative of romantic conflict where the beloved has been "pledged this very week" to another (Soneta 255). The poems progress from questioning whether to force love upon an unwilling recipient (254), to recognizing the beloved's divided loyalties (255), to urging abandonment of existing commitments for love's sake (256). The final soneta's declaration "For in claiming my name, you crown king a beggar" transforms social hierarchies through the power of love, positioning romantic commitment as capable of elevating even the lowest social position.

Hidden Waters (Sonetas 258-268)

Soneta 258: "Àsàké, what is childhood?..."

Àsàké: A Yoruba name (pronounced ah-SHAH-keh) meaning "one who is to be cherished." Yoruba is a language spoken primarily in Nigeria and parts of West Africa.

Soneta 259: "Like nuns in a nunnery, sworn to bouts of silence..."

Sworn to bouts of silence: Incorporates the practice of "Grand Silence" observed in many monastic communities, particularly Trappist orders, where members maintain complete silence for extended periods as spiritual discipline. The poem uses this religious practice to examine enforced silence in romantic and social contexts.

Soneta 261: "I want to be free. I want to succeed..."

Like Jonah in the deep, sightless, surrounded by seaweed: Draws from the biblical prophet Jonah who was swallowed by a great fish where he remained for three days and nights (Jonah 1:17-2:10). The poem transforms this biblical narrative into a powerful metaphor for psychological confinement, connecting personal despair to ancient symbolic language of entrapment and potential deliverance.

Soneta 262: "Rachel weeps for a fee, so she can feed..."

Rachel weeps: Directly invokes Jeremiah 31:15 - "Rachel weeping for her children and refusing to be comforted, because they are no more." The biblical mourning is transformed into a contemporary professional mourner who cries at funerals to support her children, creating a stark contrast between sacred grief and economic necessity.

Soneta 264: "When you're a ghetto chef, you master the art..."

Cooking crack: Examines the preparation of crack cocaine, prevalent in economically disadvantaged urban communities since the crack epidemic (1980s-1990s). The soneta presents this illegal activity as a necessary survival skill rather than a moral failing, revealing how economic desperation shapes behavior in marginalized communities. The disparity in sentencing between crack (associated with Black users) and powder cocaine (white users) has been a persistent issue in American criminal justice. The 2010 Fair Sentencing Act and subsequent First Step Act (2018) reduced this disparity, though critics note that significant differences in prosecution and sentencing outcomes remain.

Talib: Talib Kweli is a socio-conscious rapper who has dedicated his art to highlighting the urban Black experience.

Soneta 265: "I was born an inmate. Cell Block South Shore..."

South Shore: A neighborhood on Chicago's South Side that has experienced significant economic challenges and violence. The metaphor of being "born an inmate" connects to Michelle Alexander's concept of "the new Jim Crow," which identifies mass incarceration as a system of racial control that effectively designates Black Americans as second-class citizens from birth.

Inmate Number 280904: The use of a prison identification number as a birthright symbolizes how children in certain neighborhoods are tracked into the criminal justice system through over-policing, underfunded schools, and lack of economic opportunity—effectively "sentenced at birth."

Withholds libraries. Promotes penitentiaries: Contrasts educational deprivation with increased funding for incarceration, reflecting documented disparities in resource allocation between education and criminal justice systems in urban areas. This line connects to broader critiques of the "school-to-prison pipeline" that disproportionately affects children of color.

Soneta 266: "In the age of Adderall..."

Adderall: A prescription medication commonly used to treat attention deficit hyperactivity disorder (ADHD). The poem confronts the medicalization of childhood behavior and its consequences, connecting individual medical interventions to broader social control mechanisms.

Soneta 268: "The demons amongst us we know, so we baffle not..."

This soneta echoes Martin Luther King Jr.'s observation: "In the end, we will remember not the words of our enemies, but the silence of our friends." King made this statement in his 1967 "The Trumpet of Conscience" lectures, reflecting on the disappointment of white moderates and allies who remained silent during critical civil rights struggles. The poem distinguishes between three groups: open adversaries ("demons" whose opposition is expected), "fence—sitters" (those who maintain neutrality during moral crises), and supposed friends who fail to stand up in "that hour of truth." This distinction reflects King's critique in "Letter from Birmingham Jail" (1963), where he identified the "white moderate, who is more devoted to 'order' than to justice" as a greater stumbling block to freedom than explicit opponents. The image of friends as a "lifeless raft" powerfully conveys how those expected to provide support can become useless precisely when most needed.

Rising Voice (Sonetas 269-282)

Soneta 269: "We were eight years in power, despite the color..."

Eight years in power: Establishes Barack Obama's presidency (2009–2017) as a historical reference point. The phrase echoes W.E.B. Du Bois's writings about Black political participation during Reconstruction and was later used as the title of Ta-Nehisi Coates' 2017 book "We Were Eight Years in Power."

The birther: Names the "birther movement" that falsely claimed President Obama was not born in the United States and therefore ineligible for the presidency. Donald J. Trump was a prominent promoter of this conspiracy theory, demonstrating how racist narratives attempt to delegitimize Black political achievement.

Soneta 270: "Whitelash for every trespass..."

Whitelash: Term describing white backlash against racial progress, popularized after the 2016 election. The poem employs this concept to reveal the cyclical pattern of progress followed by resistance.

Stagville to Parrish Street, Colfax to Greenwood, Ocoee to Oval: Creates a historical timeline through sites of both racial violence and Black achievement: • Stagville: Former North Carolina plantation with over 900 enslaved people • Parrish Street: Durham's "Black Wall Street," a center of African American business • Colfax: Site of the 1873 massacre where 150+ Black men were killed • Greenwood: Tulsa's prosperous Black district destroyed in the 1921 massacre • Ocoee: Florida town where dozens of Black residents were killed for attempting to vote in 1920 • Oval: The Oval Office, symbolizing Obama's presidency.

Survived Charlottesville: References the 2017 "Unite the Right" rally in Charlottesville, Virginia. During this event, white supremacists, protesting the removal of a Confederate statue, marched with torches, leading to violent clashes with counter-protesters; one counter-protester, Heather Heyer, was murdered when a white supremacist deliberately drove his car into a crowd. In response to these events, then-President Donald J. Trump stated there were "very fine people on both sides," a comment that drew widespread condemnation for appearing to equate participants in the white supremacist rally with those protesting against it. This soneta's reference to "surviving Charlottesville" alludes not only to the physical violence but also to the profound moral and political crisis highlighted by such events and the ensuing national discourse, positioning it within the continuum of American racial conflict and "whitelash."

Soneta 271: "Freedom of speech ain't never been free for me..."

Citizens United: Names the 2010 Supreme Court case Citizens United v. FEC that removed restrictions on political campaign spending by corporations and organizations. The poem connects this ruling directly to the silencing of marginalized voices through the line "Moneybags so loud drowns my shriek," exposing how wealth amplifies certain voices in political discourse while rendering others inaudible.

Soneta 272: "I cain't never be woke. 'Cause to be woke..."

Strange fruit on oak tree: Invokes the history of lynching of Black Americans and directly references "Strange Fruit," Billie Holiday's 1939 song protesting lynching with the lyrics "Black bodies swinging in the southern breeze / Strange fruit hanging from the poplar trees." The poem connects historical racial violence to contemporary attempts to suppress political consciousness. The term "woke" originated in African American Vernacular English as awareness of social injustice before becoming more widely used in discussions about racial consciousness and social activism.

Soneta 273: "The meek shall inherit the earth was not spoken..."

The meek shall inherit the earth: From Jesus's Sermon on the Mount (Matthew 5:5). The soneta reinterprets this beatitude, declaring meekness not as weakness but as resilience and strength in the face of oppression. The final line, "The meek shall inherit the earth was spoken of lions," transforms conventional understanding of meekness from passivity to powerful restraint.

Soneta 274: "Six Triple Eight. Black Doves in Hitler's war..."

Six Triple Eight: The 6888th Central Postal Directory Battalion, the only all-Black, all-female battalion deployed overseas in WWII, commanded by Major Charity Adams. The battalion was finally recognized with the Congressional Gold Medal in 2022, highlighting the delayed recognition of their service. The poem reclaims this overlooked history of Black women's military service.

Charity for heart: Contains a double meaning - both the virtue of charity/love and Major Charity Adams, the battalion's commanding officer. This wordplay connects individual leadership to broader virtues.

Adams' Eve: Contains double meaning – both a nod to Adam in Genesis and the brave women led by Major Charity Adams.

Soneta 275: "We fought at Appomattox. Braved with blood the guns..."

Appomattox: Site of Confederate General Robert E. Lee's surrender to Union General Ulysses S. Grant in 1865, marking the effective end of the Civil War. Approximately 5,000 Black Union soldiers were involved in the Appomattox campaign, representing one of the largest gatherings of African American troops during the war. The poem asserts Black Americans' active role in securing their own freedom.

Fort Pillow: Site of the 1864 massacre where Confederate troops under Nathan Bedford Forrest (later a KKK founder) murdered hundreds of surrendered Black Union soldiers. This historical reference exposes the brutality faced by Black soldiers fighting for freedom.

Soneta 276: "To the rejected, the dejected, scum of the earth..."

Scum of the earth: Draws from 1 Corinthians 4:13, where Paul describes apostles as having "become as the scum of the world, the dregs of all things." The soneta repurposes this biblical language about the despised to declare their ultimate spiritual triumph, transforming social marginalization into moral authority.

Soneta 277: "Right to be free. Freedom to be right..."

Calls America to be America: Echoes Langston Hughes' poem "Let America Be America Again" (1936), which confronts the gap between American ideals and reality for marginalized people. The soneta continues Hughes' tradition of holding America accountable to its professed values.

For all lives cannot matter, while many lives are fodder: References the tension between "All Lives Matter" and "Black Lives Matter" movements, presenting a critique of claims to universal concern that fail to address specific inequities.

Soneta 278: "We want to move on, but you won't let us..."

Made you your Black holiday: References the establishment of Juneteenth (June 19) as a federal holiday in 2021, commemorating the emancipation of enslaved African Americans. The poem questions whether symbolic recognition substitutes for substantive justice.

A lady justice—without precedent: Identifies Ketanji Brown Jackson, confirmed in 2022 as the first Black woman to serve on the U.S. Supreme Court. The poem acknowledges this milestone while questioning whether representation alone constitutes progress.

Soneta 279: "What is progress?..."

Two hundred forty-six years: Measures the period from 1619 (when the first documented enslaved Africans arrived in Virginia) to 1865 (the end of the Civil War), representing the duration of American slavery. The poem uses this historical timeframe to challenge superficial definitions of progress.

Can't dig a knife ten inches / Deep in my belly, pull out an inch: Draws from Malcolm X's powerful metaphor that partial remedies to profound injustice don't constitute genuine progress. The visceral imagery reinforces the inadequacy of incremental change in response to historical atrocities.

Forty acres, mule, refuse fourfold: Connects both the unfulfilled promise made to formerly enslaved people after the Civil War—"forty acres and a mule"—and biblical principles of restitution. "Fourfold" invokes Exodus 22:1 and Zacchaeus's promise in Luke 19:8 to repay four times what he had wrongfully taken, establishing a biblical standard for meaningful reparations.

Soneta 280: "Has pain found an expiration date..."

Forebears burned in Hitler's oven: References the Holocaust (1941-1945) in which six million Jews were murdered by Nazi Germany. The soneta highlights different expectations for historical memory, revealed by the disparity between Holocaust and lynching memorials. The United States has over 300 Holocaust memorials and museums, while until recently there was no national memorial for the thousands of lynching victims. The National Memorial for Peace and Justice in Montgomery, Alabama (opened 2018) is the first major national memorial to lynching victims. This contrast exposes differing standards for which historical traumas merit public remembrance—despite growing evidence, including from the field of epigenetics, indicating that the trauma experienced by victims can have lasting, inheritable consequences for their descendants

Soneta 282: "The spirit of the Lord God is upon me..."

The spirit of the Lord God is upon me: Quotes Isaiah 61:1, a prophetic passage later read by Jesus (Luke 4:18) to announce his ministry. The soneta directly connects biblical prophetic tradition to the poet's own belief in his calling to speak out, positioning social justice work within a sacred lineage.

For He has given me the tongue of the learned: Quotes Isaiah 50:4. This passage describes prophetic eloquence divinely granted to comfort the suffering and speak truth to power.

BOOK II:
TESTAMENT

The Burning Gate

(Sonetas 283-304)

SONETA 283

Every man must do what's right in his own eyes—
Is this not Freedom's yoke upon us? We are
Sons of Liberty, and against terror we must rise:
Burn ships, pour tar on British flesh—scorch and scar.
We've cast their tea into the sea—Boston Tea Party—
Call us Patriots—not Militants. The victor writes for history.

SONETA 284

We hold these truths to be self-evident:
All men are created equal, some more equal than others;
Endowed by their Creator with certain inalienable Rights,
Wherein such, by Providence, Three-Fifths in stature, in reasoning deficient,
These Rights cannot enjoy—neither as equals, nor as brothers;
For Life, Liberty, Happiness are divine lots of the Whites.

SONETA 285

America, you have always been America.
You have always been true to the venom
Of your youth—wild like an ox that stomps
The grass of the prairie, devouring its manna.
You propose to Freedom, and her dowry condemn;
Cry *Liberty*! while the Negro, Indian, Palestinian, trump like skunks.

SONETA 286

We are the city on a hill.
The indispensable nation.
As light is to darkness, salt to the grill,
So are we to the earth, on every ocean.
Our destiny manifests: SHEPHERD THE AGE OF MEN.
No matter whom we slay, ours is amen.

SONETA 287

Our duty calls us to the West, destined to possess—
For ours is the kingdom, and the glory,
The power, and the honor, to wrestle and to wrest,
The suckling from his breast, the elder from her family,
The Mexican, the Indian, the weary and the teary;
From Mississippi to Pacific, ours is destiny, ours the territory.

SONETA 288

I'm the American man, and woman, on the wild plains
Of the Wild West, taming the tribes of the wilderness,
Claiming their land for our destiny, commanded by the Creator.
I'm the American man, and woman, on the scorched plains
Of the West Bank, *crusading* in the name of holiness.
But don't call me a Usurper. Call me a Settler.

SONETA 289

We are the People of the West; it's our portion
To be Blessed, but you cannot do as we've led,
For our destiny manifests,—said the Eagle to the Bear.
How you've savaged the Crane, like we annexed the Cession—
When we ravaged Rio Grande—for Country, God, and Homestead.
To devour another—by force—is barbaric! Yet, you dare?!

SONETA 290

I am the wild wind's roar—born upon the prairie.
The sky my roof, the earth my floor.
The water my blood, the buffalo my body.
I am Satanta, son of Kiowa,—The White Bear.
Upon this land I'll die to save my kind,
Heed or be killed—shall never bow to Bluecoat's command.

SONETA 291

Guadalupe Hidalgo, what son did you let go
To the Eagle for the sum of your sorrow?
What homes did the bird swallow? What rainbow
Did the gringo burn to shadows with his fiery ammo?
Your song was stolen. Your lungs were broken.
What more did you suffer to feed the kraken?

SONETA 292

What's the pre-existing condition of our existence?
Why must we die like flies in silence?
You label us as violent, like we've got no conscience,
Some low-grade race designed to devolve by science.
I can never tell you why you pound like giants
Stomping me and my people like ants. Damn our compliance.

SONETA 293

Shall God save the king, or maim his limbs,
Stretch his torso upon a wooden beam, whip and fill
His soul with stool from Derby's Dose—gag—so he
Cannot but choke—slit his nose—reparations for beastly sins.
From Kingston to Montego, Amity Hall to Cinnamon Hill,
Creole Negro—gwan. Break yuh yoke! Come Christmas—die free!

SONETA 294

Eighty-five bars for one buy—textile, gin, and gunpowder.
Twenty-five lives for White trader: plenty brothers for refined copper.
Abíọ́dún lures Ìyábọ́ to light dinner; Tòkunbọ́ to come chatter;
Mákindé to co-plant okra. Slowly, violently, screams turned to whimper,
Abiodun’s captives weep in the darkened monster. Shackled like critter.
Leusden, full of Black cargo, waves goodbye—till next litter.

SONETA 295

God, are you wicked? I need must ask,
For I stand at loss—astounded by the impunity
Of darkness, prosperity of vileness, rising like fall of dusk,
Swarming the dove, strangling the babe with catastrophe.
As you reasoned then, so is now: thoughts of men,
Imagination of men—continually evil. You watch brethren—eat brethren.

SONETA 296

Africa, maybe the messiah already came and is gone
And all you've got is this dust you are on.
This parched penniless stretch of earth, drenched in sun,
Cursed like one sustained by worms, from whom hope's withdrawn.
The sons are born to farm a land sorely undone;
Buried beneath her grounds rivers of gold that never run.

SONETA 297

We are not the sins of our fathers—oh, never!
Whatever they built by plunder, we've repurposed with power.
Yes, we carry their fame; must we also their blunders,
When everyone's to blame? Equity, right? Slaves, masters—equal sinners.
Whoever starts behind must gallop faster than his peer,
Or forever sink into shadows of despair. It's only fair.

SONETA 298

Many have received the things we are trying to achieve,
Bequeathed the blessings we are dying to conceive;
The many born more equal, endowed by the Creator
With many inalienable Rights—foreign to our progenitors;
Who stood upon the shore of no return, chatteled masses,
Who fought for Right to rise, despite the many lashes.

SONETA 299

The law cannot do what the law must do
For the law lies subdued by coup of power-few;
Though brawny law was made by few—sanctuary for you—
The newcomer on teeming shore, you of every hue.
Yet she lies subdued, gagged and nude, black and blue,
Betrayed anew by the very rule we all hold true.

SONETA 300

Justice for our criminals. Mercy for our convicts.
Is this not the Negro's ask? No more, no less.
Not a quarter from the poor white—his freedom restrict.
Or a penny from the brown man—his dinner possess.
Ask only that frail law be blind as raging gale,
Gentle as cooling pond, colorless for every jail, every male.

SONETA 301

I'm driving Miss Daisy tonight. Been a long day
Of getting gas, fetching mail, washing car, mowing lawn, cleaning glass—
And it's only half past noon. I once dreamed wild:
Sail the Seven Seas, engrave my name in dateless clay.
But tonight, donning my tux—service uniform for the underclass—
Miss Daisy's got soirée with pedigree—drive. park. smile. profiled.

SONETA 302

I have reinvented myself so many times—
I reckon must either become, or die becoming. Zero happenstance.
Not 'cause I'm accursed with coin, chasing quarters and dimes,
But I seek liberty of conscience, against tyranny of performance,
Conforming, laughing when I haven't been tickled, scratching this body
Where I didn't itch. I must become. Or die nobody.

SONETA 303

My pain smells, so I hide. Wear this mask
To hide the feces of my face, contain the odor
From my pain, so your dollars would not cringe, run,
Leave me in chains, if I dare refuse your ask.
So I dance, write, jump, laugh like your joker,
God forbid my mask should slip, and I be undone.

SONETA 304

It's a white man's world, so can I speak
Where I was never meant to be, breathe when
I was never meant to live? Maybe I was born
His bum to always lick, bootlicker, soulful nigger too weak,
Too dumb, to know world ain't free for colored men—
May I sing to you, sir? My supper must earn.

Fields of Salt

(Sonetas 305-316)

SONETA 305

My hands are bloody. My soul is filthy.
Sullied by the silence of my voice—guilty as Hitler.
I've deafened my ears to cries of the elderly,
Covered my eyes to the gutting of the toddler;
Pardoned Yankee bombs, Jewish gunners, cutting Arab lives in masses—
In the name of Hamas—mowing human lives like grasses.

SONETA 306

You cannot say you did not know how low
The river had run, how cold the waters have flowed.
How from the River to the Sea, fallen trees,
Like cedars of Lebanon, precious cones in each bough,
Dyed the river red—your bombs unload ... like tumors—explode.
You cannot say, GenocideJoe: *Didn't know, Gaza bleeds like seas.*

SONETA 307

My eyes are heavy, like they are drowning
Within the sockets of my soul. Weighted down by the
Burden of my sight: Babies burning in their cribs,
Mothers crying from their tombs, but nobody is counting.
Gaza lies in ruins, defaced by Hell's fury—Yankee-Israeli—
Shattered by Death's army. Punctured ribs and kids.

SONETA 308

Look at them, terrorists and jihadists, swaddled in burial white—
Gashed faces and punctured temples prayed unanswered to Allah.
Malika is six. Her sister is two. Anarchists and Extremists.
Never again, we said. *Never again shall we live a-fright,*
Burning in ghettos. So we hammered Jabalia—
Till there were no survivors. Terrorists and jihadists.

SONETA 309

Samson, let go of Gaza. Let down the tiny tot
In your hands, the toddler gasping, squirming for air
In the massive grasp of your mighty hand.
Have you come for Philistia—the honey of a harlot?
Or the flowery doorposts of Gaza, to tear her bare,
Rape her dead—leave nothing but whistling sand, barren land?

SONETA 310

Every night the sunlight dies beneath the Gazan sky
And the moonlight hides from the bombers' hum,
Children cry as darkness rises, for monsters pry
At every door, in every tent,—Boom! A wrecking drum!
400 nights of constant dark, since Zion snatched every light,
Leaving us to dine, lie, die in frightening blight.

SONETA 311

The will to kill the pen; resist this blitz
Against my will—damn this siege to pen my hopes;
Tortured thoughts that beat against my wits
Like a pugilist, dragging me against the ropes,
Till my feet can cope no more, and my hands
Shield no more, but write, then write, whatsoever it demands.

SONETA 312

I have written what I have written. Shall not waver.
Like the law of Medes that cannot be broken,
My faith is unshaken—unconquerable by any king.
I've kissed not the cheek of conscience for silver—
Bartered not my calling for lucre. And now, Hell's awoken,—
Like Daniel in lions' den, Beelzebub to my bosom cling.

SONETA 313

Ethnocracy for me. Bureaucracy for you.
Annexation for me. Occupation for you.
Security for me. Calamity for you.
Encroachment for me. Encampments for you.
What's good for goose, is never good for gander—
A homeland for Jews, dissent is slander.

SONETA 314

What have we made, what have we created?
Where on earth have we gone left, abandoned the right?
To save the Jews, we bruised the Druze,
Forbade the Arab, handmade the Nakba, our conscience propitiated.
But Democracy she's not: of Jews, for Jews—a birthright,
Cannot be right. Ethnocracy we've birthed—Liberty, strictly for Jews.

SONETA 315

Colonies on the West Bank. Tyranny on the homeland.
Massacred in our own towns. Strangers on our own land.
Hassled like cattle for slaughter. Valued like refuse for dumpster.
On a hill in Hebron, soldiers armed with mortar
Shower evening market at random: Bread. Bodies. Blood. Guts.
God and guns. Colonies on the river. Zionists on stolen blocs.

SONETA 316

WE know what it's like to not have a voice
In your own land. WE know what it's like to
Have your homes bombed, and your children burned.
WE know what it's like to boil, feel no choice
But to answer hate—with hate. WE know, this too,—
WE can never be fully free till Palestine is affirmed.

Earth's Cry

(Sonetas 317-329)

SONETA 317

Cry not for me, O barren land!
Weep not for me, O forsaken country.
Did I not cry? Did I not sigh?
Till there was no sand 'pon which to stand?
My bones for the vulture, my blood to the flea.
Alas, sorrow hacks you like axe. Weep. Cry. And die.

SONETA 318

Tulip tree, how long shall you live?
How long shall you breathe upon your golden sleeves
Deadly fumes that sap your breath, trim your years?
Were it true mortal eyes could see your many tears,
Shed in fear of your coming end. For mankind lives
To bleed the earth, till golden crowns as ashen leave.

SONETA 319

Sparks of red, dancing with olive green,
Kindle the crispy air with whistling fare,
Prancing on every tree, brightening autumn's cheer with silky brown
And orange sheen; whilst golden leaves, where verdure was queen,
Shimmer with glee, litter the streets—with silent flair.
But the cobalt sky, seething with spite, thunders his frown.

SONETA 320

Glory be to God, the forge of all works,
From whose clutch all mighty things have sprung;
Whose call awakened sunless Day from the mucks
Of formless Night, the dreary sludge of watery dung;
Who formed the god from auburn clay, in Eden placed,
Crowned him with life. O praise ye, who are graced!

SONETA 321

Subdue the earth. Fill the earth. Cease from Babel.
Were these not my summons, O son of man?
Yes, you've planted your feet upon the stars,
Broke free of gravity, yet savaged incestuously your cradle—
Sabotaged the work of my hands; strangled her lifespan.
Her blood cries out to me. Like Abel's, it roars.

SONETA 322

You cast me out of the garden, but never out
Of your Eden; for the earth is yours, the fullness,
The splendor, the wonder of your power shines forth—throughout.
Though my sin I'd covered with fig, till Christ's righteousness,
The works of your hands have you made me steward.
Alas, like Prodigal, your paradise have I wasted, wrecked, disappeared.

SONETA 323

I searched for you, and I couldn't find you—
Where did you go? I thought together were in paradise
But when did paradise, rustling leaves, become Hades for you?
When did you die—and I couldn't tell? Was wise
Once I ate the fruit, but wisdom made me foolish—
So I poached, encroached, exposed your wildlife to horrors hellish.

SONETA 324

Why is the world so broken, why are the doves
So sullen? They neither cry, nor fly, nor gather
In droves. Maybe there was a time before The Fall,
Before the doves of old were turned to wolves
And serpents lived at peace with moles. Before the nakba,
Before waters of Eden turned fountains of blood and skull.

SONETA 325

Black sparrows eating black sparrows
Makes me wanna holler—wonder what the hell
Is going on? Black birds sinking their tongues
Into their young; shooting arrows in their marrows;
Trading songs of Truth for harmonies of Hell.
Hear Marvin wailing: *mercy, mercy me*—how long, how long?

SONETA 326

I cannot say evil is destined to prevail
Because darkness covers the day.
Nor can I say evil is destined to remain
Because sunny hours of day, like gale, hurry to pale.
Evil, then, I say, is like hound seeking his prey,
It feasts when good men cease to brave his pain.

SONETA 327

Drill, baby, drill! Drill till we reach the center
Of the earth. And our summer is hell.
And our winter is red, like heat from the cremator.
Drill, baby, drill! 'Cause the science is false, cuckadodoo bonkers—
Typhoons ain't worse, hurricanes ain't close,—as you can tell.
So let's *live más*, let the oceans swell, fearmongers repel.

SONETA 328

Poetry ought to be read, silently hugged and caressed.
Poetry ought to be shared, virulently spread and dispersed.
Poetry ought to be feared, discreetly heard and confessed.
Poetry ought to be paired, like a bottle of wine,
Cellared and cooled, for a party of two, lying supine,
Beneath the sycamine, with nothing but stars, chocolate, and shoreline.

Endnotes for BOOK II: TESTAMENT

The Burning Gate (Sonetas 283-304)

Soneta 283: "Every man must do what's right in his own eyes—"

Sons of Liberty: Revolutionary-era organizations formed in the American colonies that engaged in acts of violence and intimidation against British officials and loyalists. Their tactics included "tarring and feathering" - a public torture where victims were stripped, covered in hot tar and feathers, and paraded through towns, causing severe burns and sometimes death.

Boston Tea Party: Often romanticized as a "protest," this 1773 action involved destroying private property worth approximately $1.7 million in today's currency. The soneta reveals how such acts are legitimized as patriotic when conducted by the eventual victors rather than labeled as terrorism or vandalism.

Soneta 284: "We hold these truths to be self-evident:"

We hold these truths to be self-evident: The opening phrase from the Declaration of Independence (1776), followed in the soneta by a deliberate contrast with its principles to expose the foundational contradictions in early American democracy. Inherent also is an allusion to George Orwell's Animal Farm: "all animals are born equal but some are more equal than others."

Three-Fifths: References the Three-Fifths Compromise in the U.S. Constitution (Article 1, Section 2), which counted enslaved people as three-fifths of a person for taxation and representation purposes. This compromise increased the political power of slaveholding states while institutionalizing the dehumanization of Black Americans within the nation's founding document.

Soneta 285: "America, you have always been America."

Negro, Indian, Palestinian, trump like skunks: Links domestic American racial oppression with international parallels. "Trump like skunks" creates a double meaning - both the verb "to trump" (surpass or outdo) and a reference to policies affecting these groups during the Trump administrations. The line establishes these populations as treated as unwelcome despite their rightful claims to belonging.

Soneta 286: "We are the city on a hill."

City on a hill: Phrase from John Winthrop's 1630 sermon "A Model of Christian Charity," which described the Puritan Massachusetts Bay Colony as a "city upon a hill" watched by the world. Later adopted by American political leaders, particularly Ronald Reagan, to express American exceptionalism and justify interventionist foreign policy.

The indispensable nation: Term popularized in the 1990s by U.S. Secretary of State Madeleine Albright to justify American international intervention, claiming: "If we have to use force, it is because we are America. We are the indispensable nation. We stand tall and we see further than other countries." This concept has justified unilateral military actions that often disregarded international consensus.

Soneta 287: "Our duty calls us to the West, destined to possess—"

Our duty calls us to the West: Encapsulates Manifest Destiny, the 19th-century belief that American expansion across the continent was both inevitable and divinely ordained. This ideology justified the displacement and genocide of Native Americans and the acquisition of Mexican territory. The doctrine was explicitly articulated in 1845 by journalist John L. O'Sullivan, who wrote of "our manifest destiny to overspread the continent."

Soneta 288: "I'm the American man, and woman, on the wild plains"

West Bank: Territory east of Israel proper, captured from Jordan in the 1967 Six-Day War and partially governed by the Palestinian Authority since 1994. Home to Palestinian communities and Israeli settlements considered illegal under international law according to United Nations Security Council Resolution 2334 (2016) and the International Court of Justice advisory opinion (2004).

Crusading in the name of holiness: This phrase evokes the historical Crusades (primarily 11th-13th centuries), which were religiously-motivated military campaigns initiated by European Christians often aimed at controlling territories deemed sacred. While participants often viewed these as holy wars fought for a righteous cause and divine mandate, the Crusades also involved immense violence, territorial conquest, and had lasting geopolitical consequences. The term "crusade" has since been used metaphorically to describe any zealous campaign pursued with ardent conviction, sometimes with an uncritical belief in its own righteousness. In this soneta, its use in the context of actions on the "scorched plains / Of the West Bank" is intended to be deeply ironic, highlighting how assertions of a holy or divinely ordained purpose can be used to legitimize actions that might otherwise be seen as usurpation or oppression, drawing a parallel to the self-justifying narratives often employed in historical and contemporary territorial expansions.

Settler... Colonialist: The soneta deliberately parallels American frontier expansion with Israeli settlement policies in the West Bank. Both historical processes employ similar rhetorical strategies—framing settlers as pioneers bringing civilization to "wild" territories while avoiding terms like "colonialism" that acknowledge illegitimate occupation. The poem exposes how language choices ("settler" versus "colonialist") function to legitimize territorial acquisition through displacement of indigenous populations.

Soneta 289: "We are the People of the West; it's our portion"

The Eagle to the Bear: National symbols of the United States (eagle) and Russia (bear), with "the Crane" representing Ukraine. The soneta examines the contrast between international responses to territorial expansion in different contexts.

Cession: Refers to the Mexican Cession of 1848 following the Mexican-American War, when Mexico was forced to cede approximately 525,000 square miles (55% of its pre-war territory) to the United States, including present-day California, Nevada, Utah, Arizona, New Mexico, and parts of Colorado, Wyoming, and Texas.

Rio Grande: River forming part of the U.S.-Mexico border that was central to territorial disputes during the Mexican-American War. President Polk claimed Mexican forces had shed "American blood upon American soil" when they crossed the Rio Grande, though the river's status as the border was itself contested. This pretext for war drew contemporary criticism; then-Congressman Abraham Lincoln, via his "Spot Resolutions," challenged Polk to identify the precise location of this alleged American soil, questioning the war's necessity and constitutionality. Echoing such skepticism, Ulysses S. Grant, who served in the Mexican-American War and would later become U.S. President, deemed it "one of the most unjust ever waged by a stronger against a weaker nation." He also viewed the subsequent American Civil War as a divine punishment for this national transgression.

Soneta 290: "I am the wild wind's roar—born upon the prairie."

Satanta, son of Kiowa,—The White Bear: Satanta (Set'tainte, 1820-1878) was a Kiowa war chief who resisted U.S. westward expansion. Known for his oratory and military leadership, he was eventually imprisoned at Huntsville State Penitentiary in Texas where he died under contested circumstances. His descendants have long challenged the official account of his death. His 1867 speech at Medicine Lodge peace negotiations eloquently articulated indigenous resistance: "I love to roam over the wide prairie, and when I do it I feel free and happy, but when we settle down we grow pale and die."

Bluecoat: Term used by Native Americans for U.S. Army soldiers, referring to their blue uniforms, particularly the cavalry forces that enforced westward expansion and displacement of indigenous peoples.

Soneta 291: "Guadalupe Hidalgo, what son did you let go"

Guadalupe Hidalgo: The Treaty of Guadalupe Hidalgo (1848) ended the Mexican-American War and forced Mexico to cede territories that became the American Southwest. The treaty promised rights to Mexican citizens in these territories, including protection of property and cultural rights, but these protections were routinely violated in subsequent decades as Anglo settlers established economic and political dominance in the region.

Soneta 292: "What's the pre-existing condition of our existence?"

Pre—existing condition: Creates dual reference to healthcare terminology (conditions present before obtaining insurance coverage) and scientific racism—the pseudoscientific belief that racial groups are biologically distinct and hierarchically ranked. This concept was used to justify slavery, colonization, and racial discrimination, positioning racial inferiority as a "pre-existing condition" of Black existence in white supremacist societies.

Soneta 293: "Shall God save the king, or maim his limbs,"

Derby's Dose: A brutal form of torture devised by Thomas Thistlewood, a British slave overseer in Jamaica, and named after an enslaved person called Derby. Historical records debate whether Derby was the first recipient of this punishment or the person frequently forced to carry it out on others. Documented in Thistlewood's detailed diaries, this punishment was inflicted on those who attempted escape or stole food. The torture involved beating the victim, rubbing a mixture of salt pickle, lime juice, and bird pepper into their open wounds, forcing another enslaved person to defecate into the victim's mouth, and then gagging them for four to five hours to prevent vomiting the feces.

Come Christmas—die free: References the Baptist War (Jamaica's Christmas Rebellion) of 1831-32, the largest slave uprising in the British Caribbean. Led by Samuel Sharpe, a Baptist deacon and skilled organizer, the rebellion began on December 25, 1831, when enslaved people refused to work and subsequently burned plantations. British forces killed hundreds in response, and Sharpe was executed in May 1832. Despite this, the rebellion significantly contributed to the British Slavery Abolition Act of 1833, demonstrating how Black-led resistance directly led to emancipation. Sharpe is now honored as a National Hero of Jamaica.

Soneta 294: "Eighty-five bars for one buy—textile, gin, and gunpowder."

Eighty-five bars for one buy: "Bars" functioned as both physical iron items and an abstract unit of account in the transatlantic slave trade. As a unit of value, bars created a standardized system where different European trade goods could be valued equivalently. Historical records from Bristol in the 1780s document a captain paying specifically "85 bars" for one male slave (the exact number referenced in the poem), provided not in actual iron but in equivalent textiles, weapons, and other goods. The "bar" system also created what historians call an "iron-slave cycle" in some regions, where communities needed European iron for defensive weapons against slave raiders, but to obtain that iron, they engaged in slaving themselves.

Abíọ̀dún... Ìyábọ̀... Tòkunbọ̀... Mákindé: Yoruba names representing Africans involved in the transatlantic slave trade, both as captives and as collaborators. The inclusion of these names personalizes what is often discussed in abstract terms and acknowledges the complex role of African intermediaries in the slave trade.

Leusden: A Dutch slave ship that made 10 voyages transporting enslaved Africans before sinking in 1738 near the coast of Suriname. When the ship began to sink, the crew nailed shut the hatches so the Africans couldn't escape, trapping and drowning approximately 700 enslaved Africans in the hold—one of the deadliest single incidents in the history of the Atlantic slave trade. The captain was never reprimanded or prosecuted for these murders.

Soneta 295: "God, are you wicked? I need must ask,"

As you reasoned then, so is now: thoughts of men, Imagination of men—continually evil: References Genesis 6:5 before the biblical flood: "The LORD saw that the wickedness of man was great in the earth, and that every imagination of the thoughts of his heart was only evil continually." The soneta engages with theodicy—the philosophical attempt to reconcile the existence of evil with an omnipotent, benevolent God.

This questioning of divine justice connects to the tradition of lament psalms in the Bible (particularly Psalms 10, 13, and 44), where biblical writers directly questioned God about suffering and injustice. Like these ancient texts, the soneta expresses moral outrage while still addressing God as the ultimate arbiter of justice.

Soneta 296: "Africa, maybe the messiah already came and gone"

Rivers of gold that never run: References the resource curse (or paradox of plenty)—the phenomenon that countries with abundant natural resources often experience less economic growth and worse development outcomes than countries with fewer natural resources. The Democratic Republic of Congo exemplifies this paradox, containing an estimated $24 trillion in untapped mineral resources (including gold, diamonds, cobalt, and coltan essential for electronics) yet remaining one of the world's poorest countries due to exploitation, corruption, and conflict over these resources.

Soneta 297: "We are not the sins of our fathers—oh, never!"

Equity, right? Slaves, masters—equal sinners: Critiques the false equivalence drawn between enslaved people and enslavers. The soneta challenges the myth of meritocracy embodied in phrases like "pull yourself up by your bootstraps," exposing how descendants of enslavers benefit from generational wealth and privilege while claiming descendants of the enslaved simply need to "gallop faster" despite systemic disadvantages.

Federal Reserve data consistently demonstrates the racial wealth gap has remained relatively unchanged for decades. As of 2023, the typical Black family had approximately 12-15 cents for every dollar of white family wealth, a proportion that has changed little since the 1950s despite legal reforms. Research establishes that intergenerational wealth transfer functions as the primary mechanism perpetuating this disparity, undermining claims that historical injustices no longer affect present economic realities.

Soneta 299: "The law cannot do what the law must do"

Though brawny law was made by few—sanctuary for you—: Echoes and subverts Abraham Lincoln's Gettysburg Address phrase "government of the people, by the people, for the people." The soneta reveals law's failure to achieve justice, particularly for marginalized communities, originates in its creation by the powerful for their own interests despite democratic rhetoric.

Soneta 301: "I'm driving Miss Daisy tonight. Been a long day"

Driving Miss Daisy: References the 1989 film depicting the relationship between an elderly Jewish woman and her Black chauffeur in the American South. The soneta uses this cultural reference to examine contemporary service work, race-based expectations, and deferred dreams, contrasting the speaker's aspirations ("engrave my name in dateless clay") with their reality ("service uniform for the underclass").

The poem reflects broader labor market disparities documented by the Bureau of Labor Statistics, which consistently shows Black Americans are overrepresented in service sector employment (25.2% of service occupations compared to 13.6% of the population) and experience a persistent wage gap ($0.80 earned for every dollar earned by white workers in comparable positions as of 2023).

Soneta 302: "...laughing when I haven't been tickled, scratching this body / Where I didn't itch."

These lines in the soneta—"Conforming, laughing when I haven't been tickled, scratching this body / Where I didn't itch"—directly echo a sentiment expressed by Dr. Martin Luther

King Jr. in his final speech, "I've Been to the Mountaintop," delivered on April 3, 1968. In that address, Dr. King recalled a time, as his colleague Rev. Ralph Abernathy often described it, when Black people were "just going around... scratching where they didn't itch, and laughing when they were not tickled." Dr. King then powerfully declared that "that day is all over," signifying a collective shift towards assertive self-definition and a resolute determination to claim their rightful place. The soneta's central theme of seeking "liberty of conscience, against tyranny of performance," and its ultimate resolve—"I must become. Or die nobody"—resonates deeply with this same spirit of rejecting inauthentic conformity and embracing a true, self-determined existence.

Soneta 303: "My pain smells, so I hide. Wear this mask"

This soneta addresses the psychological burden of code-switching—adjusting one's self-presentation to conform to dominant cultural expectations. This concept draws from W.E.B. Du Bois' theory of "double consciousness" in "The Souls of Black Folk" (1903), where he described the "sense of always looking at one's self through the eyes of others."

Research has documented measurable health impacts of this phenomenon. Studies from the American Psychological Association have shown that the constant vigilance required by code-switching contributes to elevated stress hormones, hypertension, and anxiety disorders. The "mask" in the poem refers not only to emotional concealment but to the physical toll of suppressing authentic expression in professional and social contexts.

Soneta 304: "It's a white man's world, so can I speak"

My supper must earn: References the historical expectation that Black Americans perform or entertain to secure economic survival. Connects to the tradition of minstrelsy and the ongoing commodification of Black culture, revealing that the speaker must "perform" acceptably to white audiences to earn basic sustenance.

Fields of Salt (Sonetas 305-316)

This section, written during the Israel-Hamas conflict that began in October 2023, addresses the humanitarian crisis in Gaza, the historical context of Israeli-Palestinian relations, and questions of moral responsibility. The sonetas engage with both immediate events and deeper historical patterns of displacement, violence, and international complicity.

Soneta 305: "My hands are bloody. My soul is dirty."

In the name of Hamas: References Hamas, the Palestinian militant and political organization which carried out an attack on Israel on October 7, 2023, killing approximately 1,200 Israelis. This soneta challenges the use of Hamas's actions as a blanket justification for the subsequent large-scale civilian casualties in Gaza.

Jewish gunners: This phrase, in the context of the soneta, alludes to the actions of Israeli military forces in Gaza. A peer-reviewed study published in The Lancet in January 2025, analyzing data up to June 30, 2024, estimated approximately 64,260 deaths in Gaza from traumatic injuries alone, noting this was likely a significant undercount and that around 59% of these deaths for which data were available were women, children, and the elderly. By early 2025, overall mortality from all conflict—related causes was understood to be far higher.

The conduct of leaders on both sides during this period drew international legal scrutiny. On November 21, 2024, the International Criminal Court (ICC) Pre-Trial Chamber I issued arrest warrants for Israeli Prime Minister Benjamin Netanyahu and then-Defense Minister Yoav Gallant, citing reasonable grounds for alleged war crimes and crimes against humanity in Gaza (including starvation as a method of warfare and intentionally directing attacks against civilians from at least October 8, 2023). Warrants were also issued for Hamas leaders (Mohammed Deif, with applications for Yahya Sinwar and Ismail Haniyeh having been withdrawn following their deaths) for alleged war crimes and crimes against humanity concerning the October 7th attacks. These ICC actions highlighted attempts to apply international law to all parties involved.

Soneta 306: "You cannot say you did not know how low"

From the River to the Sea: Phrase from Palestinian nationalist slogan "From the river to the sea, Palestine will be free," referring to the land between the Jordan River and Mediterranean Sea. Interpreted by supporters as a call for Palestinian rights throughout historic Palestine and by critics as a call for eliminating Israel.

GenocideJoe: A nickname applied to President Joe Biden by critics of U.S. support for Israel's military operations in Gaza following October 7, 2023. The U.S. provided approximately $18.3 billion in military aid to Israel between 2023-2025 (updated figure), including bombs, artillery shells, and tactical vehicles. This support continued despite multiple UN agencies, including UNICEF and the World Health Organization, issuing statements about unprecedented humanitarian impacts on civilian populations.

Soneta 307: "My eyes are heavy, like they are drowning"

Gaza lies in ruins, defaced by Hell's fury—Yankee-Israeli—: This soneta responds to the profound humanitarian crisis in Gaza. By early 2025 (data as of March 2025), the scale of devastation was immense. Reports from UN agencies and partners (such as UNRWA and OCHA, often citing figures from the Gaza Ministry of Public Works and Housing) indicated that as much as 90-92% of housing units in the Gaza Strip had been damaged or destroyed. This widespread destruction contributed to critical shortages of medical supplies, food, and water, with most hospitals non-operational and severe risks of disease outbreaks due to collapsed sanitation systems.

In February 2025, a joint Interim Rapid Damage and Needs Assessment (IRDNA) by the World Bank Group, the United Nations, and the European Union estimated overall recovery and reconstruction needs for Gaza and the West Bank at approximately $53.2 billion over the subsequent decade, with around $30 billion accounting for direct damages to physical infrastructure in Gaza alone. These figures underscored the conflict as causing one of the most intensive destruction rates of the 21st century.

Soneta 308: "Look at them, terrorists and jihadists, swaddled in burial white—"

Jabalia: Jabalia Refugee Camp, the largest of Gaza's eight refugee camps, established in 1948. In late 2023 and early 2024, it experienced heavy bombardment during the Israel-Hamas war, with multiple strikes killing dozens of civilians, including children. The camp, housing over 110,000 registered refugees (according to UNRWA data prior to the conflict) within an area of just 1.4 square kilometers, possesses an extreme population density that made it particularly vulnerable to high casualty rates during bombardment.

Soneta 309: "Samson, let go of Gaza. Let down the tiny tot"

Samson... Gaza: Biblical reference to Judges 16, where Samson, captured by Philistines, destroyed the temple in Gaza, killing both himself and his captors. The poem creates a parallel to modern Gaza, portraying Israel as becoming like Samson in its destructive power.

Soneta 310: "Every night the sunlight dies beneath the Gazan sky"

400 nights of constant dark, since Zion snatched every light: References Gaza's severe electricity crisis, catastrophically exacerbated by the conflict from October 2023. Even before this, Gaza often received only 8-12 hours of electricity daily due to restrictions and infrastructure issues. Post-conflict, a near-total blackout ensued as Israeli authorities cut supply and Gaza's power plant depleted fuel. By early 2025, reports indicated around 80% of Gaza's power infrastructure was destroyed, forcing widespread reliance on generators for scarce power. In March 2025, the

situation worsened as reports indicated Israel cut power to the last Gaza facility receiving it from the Israeli grid.

Soneta 313: "Ethnocracy for me. Bureaucracy for you."

Ethnocracy: A political structure where one ethnic group dominates the political system, contrasted with democracy where equal rights are theoretically extended to all citizens regardless of ethnicity. The term was formalized by political scientist, and Israeli, Oren Yiftachel to describe systems where ethnic affiliation, rather than citizenship status, determines access to rights and resources.

The soneta's structure—presenting paired opposing concepts ("Ethnocracy for me. Bureaucracy for you." "Annexation for me. Occupation for you.")—reveals the disparate treatment of different populations under the same governmental system. Each line presents a favorable condition "for me" juxtaposed with its oppressive counterpart "for you," exposing systemic inequality through this parallel construction.

A homeland for Jews, dissent is slander: Addresses accusations that criticism of Israeli policies is automatically antisemitic. The line demonstrates that legitimate criticism of the state of Israel is often dismissed as prejudice against Jewish people, conflating the nation-state with the religious/ethnic identity. For many, it has become known as the Great Silencer.

Soneta 314: "What have we made, what have we created?"

Nakba: Arabic for "catastrophe," referring to the 1948 mass displacement and dispossession of Palestinians during Israel's establishment. Between 700,000-750,000 Palestinians fled or were expelled from their homes, over 500 Palestinian villages and towns were destroyed, and Palestinians lost control of approximately 78% of historic Palestine. The event remains central to Palestinian collective memory and identity, with many refugee families still possessing keys to homes they left behind.

Druze: A religious and ethnic minority present in Israel, Syria, Lebanon, and Jordan. In Israel, Druze citizens serve in the military but have also experienced discrimination, creating a complex position within Israeli society.

This soneta also references Israel's "Basic Law: Israel as the Nation-State of the Jewish People" (2018), which defined Israel as "the national home of the Jewish people," established Hebrew as the sole official language (downgrading Arabic from "official" to "special status"), and declared "Jewish settlement as a national value." The law generated significant controversy both internationally and within Israel, with a dissenting opinion from an Israeli Supreme Court justice highlighting concerns about discrimination against non-Jewish citizens. Even the

10-judge majority that upheld the law in 2021 acknowledged that "it would have been better if the principle of equality had been explicitly enshrined" in it.

Soneta 315: "Colonies on the West Bank. Tyranny on the homeland."

The soneta addresses Israeli settlements in the West Bank, which have expanded significantly since Israel captured the territory in 1967. As of early 2025, approximately 700,000 Israeli settlers lived in the West Bank and East Jerusalem in settlements considered illegal under international law by the United Nations Security Council Resolution 2334 (2016) and the International Court of Justice advisory opinion (2004).

Soneta 316: "WE know what it's like to not have a voice"

This soneta draws parallels between various experiences of oppression, asserting solidarity between different marginalized groups. The capitalized "WE" creates ambiguity about which specific group is speaking, allowing multiple readings depending on which historical context readers bring to the poem.

Earth's Cry (Sonetas 317-329)

Soneta 321: "Subdue the earth. Fill the earth. Cease from Babel."

Subdue the earth. Fill the earth: Commands from Genesis 1:28, where God instructs humans to "be fruitful and multiply, fill the earth and subdue it." The soneta reimagines these as ecological warnings rather than permissions for exploitation.

Babel: References Genesis 11:1-9, where humans attempted to build a tower to reach heaven, resulting in God confusing their languages and scattering them across the earth. The story serves as a warning against human hubris.

Soneta 322: "You cast me out of the garden, but never out"

Cast me out of the garden... Eden: Alludes to Genesis 3:23-24, where Adam and Eve are expelled from the Garden of Eden. The soneta reimagines this as humanity's failure of environmental stewardship rather than simple disobedience.

Soneta 324: "Why is the world so broken, why are the doves"

Before The Fall: References the theological concept from Genesis 3 when humans disobeyed God and were expelled from Eden, bringing sin and death into the world.

Nakba: By placing this Arabic term for the Palestinian catastrophe alongside biblical references to "The Fall," the soneta creates a parallel between theological fall from grace and historical displacement, establishing both as profound ruptures in human experience.

Soneta 325: "Black sparrows eating black sparrows"

Makes me wanna holler: References Marvin Gaye's 1971 song "Inner City Blues (Makes Me Wanna Holler)" which addresses urban poverty and environmental degradation.

What the hell is going on: Echoes a line from Marvin Gaye's "What's Going On" (1971), his landmark social consciousness album addressing environmental and social issues.

Marvin wailing: mercy, mercy me: References Marvin Gaye's 1971 environmental protest song "Mercy Mercy Me (The Ecology)," which laments pollution and environmental degradation with the line "things ain't what they used to be."

Soneta 327: "Drill, baby, drill! Drill till we reach the center"

Drill, baby, drill: Political slogan popularized by Republican vice-presidential candidate Sarah Palin during the 2008 U.S. presidential campaign, advocating for increased domestic oil drilling.

According to the IPCC (Intergovernmental Panel on Climate Change) AR6 report from 2021 and subsequent global temperature monitoring, average global temperatures have increased by approximately 1.3°C above pre-industrial levels as of early 2025. NOAA data shows that 2024 set records for global ocean temperatures, sea level rise, and frequency of Category 4-5 hurricanes. The soneta's ironic deployment of "the science is false" contradicts the overwhelming scientific consensus on anthropogenic climate change and its measurable impacts.

Let's live mas: References Taco Bell's advertising slogan "Live Más" (Live More), introduced in 2012. The soneta ironically juxtaposes this consumptive corporate messaging with environmental destruction, revealing how commercial culture encourages hedonistic consumption despite ecological consequences.

SANCTUARY

(THE INTERLUDE)

There are places I want to go where tomorrow
Is only a day old. Undisturbed. Unreinforced. Undeformed.
No chatter of heavy chain-saw mills blasting like stereo
But rows of marigold, perfumed and yellow. Uniformed. Adorned.
Where heaven meets earth, and bluish whitish clouds
Meet bluish greenish sea, far from the maddening crowds.

BOOK III:
THE RECKONING

Falling Towers

(Sonetas 329-339)

SONETA 329

The center has fallen! The center has fallen!
Lucifer crawls across the Deep. The Crypt is open.
Abyss is awoken. The Seal is broken.
Darkness feasts upon the face of man. Tears the land.
Hear me, hear me, you damned! Who withstands my hand?
Yours was the republic, yours could not keep. Wretched wasteland!

SONETA 330

New rules for old rules. Steel noose for cotton noose.
Heard on the evening news: Poogie died on Old Moose.
Parked for short snooze. Fried from morning bruise.
BANG! BANG!! Copman on glass. Sir, are you on booze?
Confused. Accused. Poogie pulls tilted seat. Fastens vintage shoes.
Rat-tat-tat! Steel noose. Same rules. Black man on evening news.

SONETA 331

We have come this far, cannot go farther,—
The tides of justice have turned, dogs of war unmoored.
The gains we've made, the same must barter
For safety and sorrow,—for speaking, many are scorned, deplored.
Countrymen, if we must die, let's not die as hogs,
Cornered, condemned; but live to show Black lives as gods.

SONETA 332

There shall be blood. Not the blood of martyrs
Fighting for justice, or seeking to keep freedom alive.
Or soldiers lost in some far-flung country, marching on orders,
Jumping in senseless graves, on plenty doubt, so medals derive.
There shall be blood. Blood of a nation,—like plague,—
Spilling its streets, withering its roots. American Carnage.

SONETA 333

Martin! Martin! Wake up! Wake up! What you wanted said,
But couldn't say, before they shot you dead?
Sermon on the Mount: *Why America May Go To Hell.*
Been sixty years since you slumped, felled, in Lorraine Motel.
Fifteen cents on the dollar still for Negro in America—
Like Vietnam, butchered Gaza. Wake up, Martin! America in Gehenna.

SONETA 334

How is it I am so blind and cannot see?
Yet in my bleakest mind deeply know, feel the weight
Of the world upon me—cross of those before me.
In the hazy maze of my days, my soul deflates,
And I lose all faith. Alone in my woeful state,
Battling all hate. Till Blackness cries: *Child, Arise! Victory awaits.*

SONETA 335

It is not that I am void of ambition,
In love with my profession, or have no compassion
For the struggling mother burdened on the journey home;
I'm ashamed of my demons, they make me loathsome.
But her pay must swipe to bake my daily bread.
In Lagos, you damn the bled, or join the dead.

SONETA 336

God save us from the tyranny of thought,
The malady, of course, that we our own dear course
Can best allot, brought to bear,—without His plot.
In times of war, in times of peace, in fraught discourse,
In one accord, may this always be our solemn lust:
No matter the cross, or cost, in God we trust.

SONETA 337

There was no appetite to save the state
For we have made so many mistakes—nailed the saints
To the stakes, cleared the way for hate to prevail,
Razed the sails. When the devil came for the gate,
To shake the frames, raise his flames—erase constraints,
The pain was great—like a mother crushed in travail.

SONETA 338

Impotent witnesses standing on the banks of the River Jordan,
Complicit in the gashing of our own souls. Like gluttons
Overtaken by stupor, overcome by the folly of our bargain—
Barabbas for Jesus, devil we know against all cautions.
Helpless, we now plead—this nation, under God, new birth
Of freedom shall breathe—and not perish from the earth.

SONETA 339

The governor's house is filled with cash from morning meetings,
Contracts na for light, drugs, plenty water, jobs to produce,
But dues don already go out. My broda, nothing treasonous,
At all, watch person suffer, as man dey chop winnings.
There are no rules, only ruse: be used or refuse—
Whatever you choose, there're no jewels for fools in Lagos.

Tongues of Fire

(Sonetas 340-353)

SONETA 340

A poem is like language. But with dialects.
A poem knows what it shall be, what shall speak:
Whether prose, sonnet, verse so free recollects
Years of all has been, or will be yet unique.
Poem is an unsung song, a soneta, a budding rose
That stirs the soul with words no tongue yet knows.

SONETA 341

The critic wishes to parse my work,
Like a miner armored with torch,
Trudging a darkened hall, blinded at every fork,
Tell where my treasure lurks, where my pleasures merge.
Alas, the critic isn't me. Nor ever could be.
So he wanders my mind, wondering at every simile.

SONETA 342

I would the world my work reward
While yet my corpse—my prideful lungs—has not consumed.
While yet my words are not some distant chord
Of a lonely dirge sung alone by the dearly entombed.
I wished the world my greatness would see,
Blindness would cease, before my soul's adrift with the sea.

SONETA 343

What shall the quill write of me when I'm done?
What shall I have bequeathed this loveless world?
Shall it be said I left without a thud?
Without so much a voice that rang like a gun,—
Blast through ages like a song that can't be recalled?
Lo! I shall write—though the world riles my blood.

SONETA 344

The truest worth of things cannot be seen
Till they've heaved their last breath. For Death himself
Heralds the sparkling spright of a star concealed;
Like a shooting star—falling from heaven's lair, hitherto unseen,—
Showers nightly sky like thousand lanterns on a lustrous shelf.
For brightest things blaze fullest when their fates are sealed.

SONETA 345

Since I did not go to school, did not know
I should. Or couldn't. Or would have written
My pleading in flora so formal my education should show;
Would have stricken my feelings—with a bludgeon smitten
My deepest dealings, so metaphors cannot mix, cultures cannot breed.
Alarmingly, ignorance is me. So I grow uncultured like weed.

SONETA 346

Mine hands have wrought what the AI could not write—
The learned scholar who sometimes lies, hides behind the guise
Of proper nouns, proper sounds, proper lines, frowns upon
My jagged rhymes, violent mimes, tells me my fight
Is far too bright: *use some subtler light,—standardize, sensitize.*
Alas, the AI never mourned, burned, or lost its sun.

SONETA 347

No one can teach the quill to write, my son,
The same way no one could teach you
How to be—teach your legs to quiver and run
When danger lurches at your door. Or stand true,
And fight, when he reaches to seize your right.
No one teaches the bird to fly—so, just write.

SONETA 348

No good poet's work ever arrives the way
Was first whispered. No telling of the divine
Ever rings so loud at first hearing. For God speaks
In murmurs, while man, shackled to tremors of toilful day
Must still himself, like a duck upon quiet pond, refine,
Furiously, till his lines align with what heaven truly seeks.

SONETA 349

Simplicity is not the opposite of complexity, Àníkẹ́ tells Àsàbí,
Before she devoured the spicy bowl of rice
She had just stewed. *You try hard to be wise,*
And layer density with profundity, boiling chemistry with biology,
So your gallery can say you're witty; the bully,
You're brainy. In clarity and brevity, wisdom hits hardest, Àsàbí.

SONETA 350

Ignorance would ban Knowledge.
So invites Hatred to disband Enlightenment:
Burn every book, tear every wall, shred every class assignment,—
So Knowledge could never rise, and Truth acknowledge.
But Truth suppressed is like spring recoiled, pressured,
Destined for Freedom,—ERUPTS! With force that cannot be censured.

SONETA 351

Whose son shall read my words, or credence give
My works, when my sun's done and shines no more.
Which daughter of Eve my verse shall cleave
To her breasts, smother with care, till my rhymes purr,
My lines roar like a cuddly beast wrapped in love.
What world shall my word live? Lionized. Unspoken of.

SONETA 352

Wakeful I lay, mine eyes in slumber would not partake
For fear of today, in dread of tomorrow.
Mine eyes, weary of things it cannot unsee,
Spend the day praying my mind its place would take,—
Mind to see, eyes to rest,—for thus, Sorrow,
Robbed of sight and mind to think, ceases to be.

SONETA 353

In my mind I wrestle with the tiger of thought.
It won't let go, and I cannot let it go
For fear it will strangle me, cut deep and gut
My soul with fiery claws, bloody teeth like crimson snow.
Yet has He made it so: Men should breathe free,
Choose the poison, or blessing, that feeds their vanity.

Blood Memory

(Sonetas 354-365)

SONETA 354

You took up arms against these States
Launched your thunder upon Fort Sumter—denounced the sacred name
That made us kin: the United States of America.
Yet, across these States, your coward name reincarnates
On schoolyards and streetlights—monuments to hate, treachery, and shame—
Altars to monsters who abhorred Blackness, from Mississippi to Alabama.

SONETA 355

We lost the war but never lost our power;
You thought us crushed but only fueled our anger.
Damn the nigger! He shall never, ever, rise to power.
We are the United Daughters of the Confederacy,
Ku Klux Klan, sovereign keepers of white pedigree, divine supremacy—
Negro's nightmare: from Black Codes to Jim Crow, bestowed legacy.

SONETA 356

Whether in heaven or in hell—Dear Andy,
The good Lord shall tell where your wretched soul
Shall rest—or yell. To you were hopes of Liberty,
Precious new birth of freedom commended. Yet, like coal
Upon a hateful fire, burned freedom's child in Confederate flames;
Reconstructed hell on earth, damned the Negro, again, to chains.

SONETA 357

You are an angry people. Lazy. Dirty. Addicted to incompetence.
Living like violence were your pedigree; White man, your boogeyman.
You struggle to level up, like White man were Superman.
Boogeyman. Superman. Sorry I've squandered your tolerance. Pardon my ignorance.
Without inheritance, opulence—whitelisted by forefathers—defended by Klan—
I've been happy with your thuggery: redlined, denied, confined. Subhuman.

SONETA 358

Judas and the Black Messiah, crucified like a Black pariah,
To fulfill the White Agenda: **Blacks can't climb the ladder.**
So they tracked the Panther, demonized the brothers,
Propagated betrayal,—Hoover and his band of hunters.
Till they got Messiah! Drugged him like critter. *Rat-a-tat-tat!*
Judas and the Black Messiah, double-crossed by naked mole rat.

SONETA 359

You rose upon the ladder we laid
Bearing yourself up upon the sacrifice we've paid.
You raged and flailed, afraid your name could never
Persuade—your claims would never dissuade—never silence your accuser.
So you railed: *This is high-tech lynching!* Summoned your race.
You made it. Seated. Denounced your race. Thomas with whiteface.

SONETA 360

Mtu Mweupe Karibu! White man, you are welcome.
And so began our Trail of Tears. Though Mtu Mweupe
Has come and gone, he's never truly left our shores—
He sits in our tongue whenever we speak at home,
We wear his clothes whenever we work and play—
He ties our hands, so can never close the doors.

SONETA 361

We can never forget, nor should we ever accept—
You took us in chains, carried us away in pain
Came back to saddle us, again, in our own lands.
Lumumba cried and tried, sought our freedoms to protect,
Fought so our children would never wear your chains—again.
You killed him. White man, show me your bloody hands!

SONETA 362

At times I feel the night is so dark
Forces so large, stars have gone black
Madness is all around, demons have won out.
My soul is burned out, strung out, in starless drought.
For all ears are deaf, all hearts are seared,
Like a suckling child, drowning in screams, but is unheard.

SONETA 363

My life is a prophecy I could not foretell,
Nor could I from the bowels of the universe
Forewarn what winds from hell should cast a spell
Upon my hoary head; nor what fairy with sweet verse
Plant her dust upon my palm to make rain appear.
I heard I hailed from somewhere, pitiful Son of Nowhere.

SONETA 364

Wicked winds did shake the tranquil figs of May,
Fierce gale did break the fancy deeds of clay.
It was the worst of times, crushing fogs of crime
Spread across the fallen realm, like fields filled with mines.
A time that tried, then broke, the souls of men,
Damned them to hell, turned them to beasts without den.

SONETA 365

When hope is gone, god becomes the opium
Of the poor—petty trader, cocoa farmer, government worker.
Sermons on Mondays, Tuesdays, Wednesdays, Fridays, Sundays,
Follow god for answers, magic wand from podium—
Preacherman is messiah, miracle worker, holy hustler of wonder.
The flock of Lagos like sheep for slaughter—praying … someday.

Endnotes for BOOK III: THE RECKONING

Falling Towers (Sonetas 329-339)

Soneta 329: "The center has fallen! The center has fallen!"

The center has fallen: Directly echoes W.B. Yeats' influential poem "The Second Coming" (1919) with its line "Things fall apart; the centre cannot hold," which depicts societal collapse. Yeats wrote during the aftermath of World War I and the Spanish flu pandemic, depicting a world descending into chaos. The soneta transforms this modernist vision of collapse to address contemporary institutional and moral breakdown.

Lucifer crawls across the Deep... The Seal is broken: Employs apocalyptic imagery from the Book of Revelation. "The Deep" references Genesis 1:2 ("darkness was upon the face of the deep") while the breaking of seals comes from Revelation 6, where the opening of seven seals heralds the apocalypse. This biblical apocalyptic language emerges historically during periods of severe social upheaval and perceived moral crisis.

Soneta 330: "Steel Noose"

"Steel noose for cotton noose" evokes the enduring evolution of racial terror in America—from the forced labor of the plantation, to the lynching rope of Jim Crow, to the steel weapons of modern policing. "Poogie," a composite figure, stands for Black men like Amadou Diallo, Walter Scott, and Philando Castile—each unarmed, each presumed guilty. The internal rhyme chain—noose, Moose, bruise, booze, shoes, news—mirrors the cyclical spectacle of Black death.

Soneta 331: "We have come this far, cannot go farther,—"

Dogs of war unmoored: References Shakespeare's Julius Caesar: "Cry 'Havoc!,' and let slip the dogs of war," a phrase establishing that once violence begins, it cannot easily be controlled. The classical allusion places contemporary American violence within a historical tradition of civil strife.

If we must die, let's not die as hogs: Directly echoes Claude McKay's influential sonnet "If We Must Die" (1919), written during the "Red Summer" of anti-Black violence. McKay's poem urged: "If we must die, let it not be like hogs... Like men we'll face the murderous, cowardly pack." The poem became a rallying cry during the Harlem Renaissance and later civil rights movements, embodying dignified resistance in the face of racial violence.

Soneta 332: "There shall be blood. Not the blood of martyrs"

American Carnage: Phrase from Donald J. Trump's 2017 inaugural address where he described "American carnage" of "crime and gangs and drugs." The soneta repurposes this phrase to reveal a different kind of national bloodshed – the internal violence resulting from political division rather than the external threats emphasized in the original speech. The inaugural address marked a significant rhetorical departure from traditional inaugural optimism, focusing instead on "rusted-out factories scattered like tombstones across the landscape" and "the crime and gangs and drugs that have stolen too many lives."

Soneta 333: "Martin! Martin! Wake up! Wake up!"

Sermon on the Mount: Why America May Go To Hell: References an undelivered sermon Martin Luther King Jr. reportedly planned before his assassination, addressing economic inequity. King focused increasingly on economic justice and poverty in his final years, arguing that racial equality without economic justice would leave fundamental problems unresolved.

Lorraine Motel: Memphis, Tennessee location where Martin Luther King Jr. was assassinated on April 4, 1968, now part of the National Civil Rights Museum. King was in Memphis supporting striking sanitation workers when he was killed.

Fifteen cents on the dollar: Reveals the persistent wealth gap between Black and white Americans. According to the Federal Reserve's 2022 Survey of Consumer Finances (the most recent comprehensive data available by early 2025), the typical Black family had approximately $44,900 in wealth compared to approximately $285,000 for the typical white family—roughly 15 cents on the dollar. This gap has remained relatively consistent for decades despite various economic changes, demonstrating the persistence of structural economic inequality.

Like Vietnam, butchered Gaza: Establishes a direct parallel between the Vietnam War (1955-1975), where American military intervention resulted in approximately 2 million civilian casualties, and the Gaza conflict that began in October 2023, where casualty figures reached into the tens of thousands. Both conflicts demonstrate patterns of overwhelming force applied against civilian populations.

Soneta 334: "How is it I am so blind and cannot see?"

This soneta explores the paradox of understanding injustice intellectually while struggling to fully comprehend its scope. The poem's final line, "Till Blackness calls: Child, Arise! Victory awaits," draws from the tradition of Black liberation theology, which interprets Christian scripture through the lens of justice for the oppressed. This tradition, developed by theologians like James Cone in the 1960s, positions God as actively engaged in the struggle against racial oppression.

Soneta 335: "It is not that I am void of ambition,"

Lagos: Nigeria's largest city with 17.2 million residents (2025), contributing about 22% of Nigeria's GDP. Despite its economic significance, Lagos presents stark contrasts: while the World Bank reports a low 4.5% extreme poverty rate, the Lagos State Government indicates nearly 80% of households experience broader poverty by local standards. With 45% of workers in the informal sector earning roughly $2-4 USD daily, the economic desperation described in the poem reflects daily reality for many residents despite the city's status as Africa's second-largest economy.

In Lagos, you damn the bled, or join the dead: Articulates the harsh economic reality where survival often requires participation in exploitative systems. "The bled" refers to those who are economically exploited, while the stark ultimatum captures the limited options available to many urban Nigerians caught between ethical compromises and destitution.

Soneta 336: "God save us from the tyranny of thought,"

In God we trust: Official motto of the United States, appearing on U.S. currency since 1864 and officially adopted by Congress in 1956 during the Cold War as part of a broader emphasis on American religious identity in contrast to "godless communism." The soneta presents this phrase as a statement of national faith amidst conflict.

Soneta 337: "There was no appetite to save the state"

This soneta examines the dissolution of democratic institutions and civic commitment. The phrase "when the devil came for the gate" crystallizes the common pattern of democratic decline identified by political scientists – where institutional guardrails are gradually weakened before more overt authoritarian measures are introduced. The poem's imagery of gradual institutional failure aligns with scholarly research on democratic backsliding, which identifies erosion of democratic norms, delegitimization of political opposition, and weakening of accountability mechanisms as key warning signs that precede more visible democratic collapse.

Soneta 339: "The governor's house is filled with cash from morning meetings,"

Written in Nigerian Pidgin English, a creole language widely spoken in Nigeria that combines English with local languages and has its own grammatical structures. The poem confronts political corruption in Lagos, Nigeria, where government officials enrich themselves while citizens suffer. "My broda" means "my brother," a common term of address. "Nothing treasonous, at all, watch person suffer" ironically notes that observing suffering without action is considered acceptable, while challenging corruption might be labeled treasonous. The final line demonstrates that in Lagos, expecting ethical governance is considered foolish, reflecting widespread disillusionment with political leadership.

Tongues of Fire (Sonetas 340-353)

Soneta 340: "A poem is like language. But with dialects."

This soneta presents a poetic manifesto, defining the nature and purpose of poetry. The comparison of a poem to "language with dialects" establishes poetry as specialized forms of communication with their own rules and expressions. The reference to a poem as "a unsung song, a soneta, a budding rose" positions this collection's innovative form (the soneta) within poetic tradition while emphasizing its organic, evolving nature.

Soneta 342: "I would the world my work reward"

This soneta articulates the universal desire for recognition during one's lifetime rather than posthumous acclaim. The phrase "While yet my corpse my prideful lungs has not consumed" creates a striking image of mortality, while the final lines express the fear that one's creative legacy might become "a lonely dirge sung alone by the dearly entombed." The poem connects to the historical pattern of artists who achieved recognition only after death, including figures like Emily Dickinson, Vincent van Gogh, and Franz Kafka.

Soneta 343: "What shall the quill write of me when I'm done?"

The soneta employs the classical metaphor of the quill (writing instrument) as the arbiter of historical legacy, questioning what will remain of the poet's voice after death. The image of a voice that "rang like a gun" captures the desire for impactful expression that resonates beyond the writer's lifetime. The final line declares the determination to write despite a hostile world ("though this world riles my blood"), reflecting the persistence necessary for artistic creation in difficult circumstances.

Soneta 344: "The truest worth of things cannot be seen"

This soneta establishes that true value emerges only at the end of something's existence, comparing this revelation to a shooting star that becomes visible only as it falls. The paradox that "brightest things blaze fullest when their fates are sealed" connects to both natural phenomena and human legacies, demonstrating that full appreciation often comes only after something is lost or completed.

Soneta 345: "Since I did not go to school, did not know"

This soneta challenges academic gatekeeping and formal constraints in poetry. The ironic reference to writing "in flora so formal my education should show" exposes conventional expectations of poetic language, while the final line's self-description as "uncultured like weed" reclaims a derogatory term as a symbol of authentic, unrestrained expression. The poem refutes the assumption that formal education is necessary for meaningful artistic expression.

Soneta 346: "Mine hands have wrought what the AI could not write—"

AI could not write: Confronts the limitations of artificial intelligence text generation systems. By 2025, AI language models had advanced significantly beyond their 2020 predecessors, becoming increasingly sophisticated at mimicking human writing styles and structures. However, as the soneta declares, these systems "never mourned, burned, or lost its sun," highlighting the fundamental gap between algorithmic pattern recognition and lived human experience that persists even in advanced systems. This critique addresses ongoing debates about whether AI-generated content constitutes actual creativity or merely sophisticated mimicry. While 2025 AI systems can produce technically proficient poems that simulate established styles, they cannot authentically convey emotions or experiences they have not—and cannot—experience.

Soneta 347: "No one can teach the quill to write, my son,"

This soneta contrasts formal instruction with innate creativity and survival instinct. The analogy between writing and instinctive physical responses to danger ("teach your legs to quiver and run / When danger lurches at your door") establishes authentic expression as arising from internal necessity rather than external instruction. The final line, "No one teaches the bird to fly—so, just write," frames artistic expression as a natural capability that needs freedom more than guidance.

Soneta 348: "No good poet's work ever arrives the way"

This soneta addresses the process of poetic creation, contrasting initial inspiration ("first whispered") with the arduous work of refinement. The image of a poet as "a duck upon quiet pond" that must "furiously" refine its work beneath the surface draws on Ernest Hemingway's iceberg theory that good writing shows only the visible portion of the author's knowledge and effort. The poem validates the necessity of revision and careful craft in creating work that ultimately appears effortless.

Soneta 349: "Simplicity is not the opposite of complexity, Àníkẹ́ tells Àsàbí,"

Àníkẹ́ and Àsàbí: Yoruba names from southwestern Nigeria. Àníkẹ (pronounced ah-NEE-kay) means "one to be cherished" while Àsàbí (pronounced ah-SAH-bee) refers to one who was carefully selected. The conversation between these characters delivers the poem's central wisdom about clarity in expression.

The soneta presents a dialogue on the nature of effective communication, warning against confusing complexity with depth ("layer density with profundity, boiling chemistry with biology"). The concluding wisdom—"In clarity and brevity, wisdom hits hardest"—delivers a stylistic manifesto that the soneta form itself embodies with its constraints of six lines and ten words per line.

Soneta 350: "Ignorance would ban Knowledge."

Burn every book, tear every wall, end every class assignment: Addresses contemporary book banning and educational restrictions in various U.S. states. According to PEN America, close to 16,000 instances of book bans occurred in U.S. school districts between 2021-2024, with a dramatic 200% increase during the 2023-2024 school year alone (10,046 instances affecting 4,231 unique titles). Books addressing race (44% featuring characters of color), LGBTQ+ issues (39% featuring LGBTQ+ characters), and sexual education are most frequently targeted. While the American Library Association documented a 65% increase in book challenges between 2022 and 2023, challenges have begun declining in 2024. Florida and Iowa have recorded the highest numbers of bans, with over 4,500 and 3,600 book bans respectively during the 2023-2024 school year.

Soneta 351: "Whose son shall read my words, or credence give"

This soneta contemplates the poet's legacy and future readership, questioning who will appreciate the work "when my sun's done and shines no more." The dual meaning of "sun/son" creates ambiguity about whether the poem addresses literal descendants or future readers. The animal imagery—a "cuddly beast wrapped in love" that will both "purr" and "roar"—portrays the poet's hope for work that can be both gentle and powerful, intimate and public.

Soneta 352: "Wakeful I lay, mine eyes in slumber would not partake"

This soneta examines insomnia caused by overwhelming awareness—"My eyes, weary of things it cannot unsee." The paradoxical wish for "mind to see, eyes to rest" expresses a desire to maintain awareness while escaping the pain of constant witness. The final line declares that "Sorrow, / Robbed of sight and mind to think, ceases to be," positioning consciousness itself as both the source of and potential escape from suffering.

Blood Memory (Sonetas 354-365)

Soneta 354: "You took up arms against these States"

Fort Sumter: Federal fort in Charleston Harbor, South Carolina where Confederate forces opened fire on April 12, 1861, beginning the American Civil War. The attack represented a direct military challenge to federal authority.

Across these States, your coward name reincarnates / On schoolyards and streetlights: Condemns the prevalent naming of U.S. public spaces after Confederate figures, often rooted in the Jim Crow era and seen as endorsing white supremacy. Despite some removals after 2020, data by early 2025 (e.g., from the Southern Poverty Law Center's "Whose Heritage?" project) indicated well over 150 public schools, over 100 counties/cities, and hundreds of highways/roads still bore such names. The poem defines these as "monuments to hate, treachery, and shame."

Soneta 355: "We lost the war but never lost our power;"

United Daughters of the Confederacy: Founded in 1894, this women's organization spearheaded Confederate memorialization via monuments, textbooks, and public commemorations. The UDC significantly shaped Southern historical education, promoting textbooks that depicted slavery as benevolent and secession as constitutionally justified, not treasonous. Between 1900-1930, the UDC was instrumental in erecting hundreds of Confederate monuments (with some estimates over 700 linked to their efforts or influence) and successfully lobbied for curricula promoting "Lost Cause" mythology.

Ku Klux Klan: White supremacist terrorist organization founded after the Civil War to violently oppose Reconstruction and Black civil rights. The soneta exposes these organizations as ensuring white supremacy continued despite Confederate military defeat, shifting from battlefield dominance to cultural, legal, and terroristic control.

Black Codes to Jim Crow: Black Codes were restrictive laws passed immediately after the Civil War to control freed Black people; Jim Crow laws formalized segregation and disenfranchisement from the 1870s through the 1960s. These legal mechanisms enforced racial subordination after slavery's formal end, demonstrating the adaptability of white supremacy following military defeat.

Soneta 356: "Whether in heaven or in hell—Dear Andy,"

Dear Andy: Refers to Andrew Johnson, who succeeded Abraham Lincoln as president after his assassination. Johnson opposed key elements of Reconstruction, vetoed civil rights legislation, and allowed former Confederate states to establish Black Codes restricting freedmen's rights. His lenient approach to former Confederate states enabled the rapid return of white supremacist governance and undermined attempts to establish meaningful citizenship rights for formerly enslaved people.

Reconstructed hell on earth: Indicts the failure of Reconstruction (1865-1877) to secure equal rights for Black Americans, culminating in the Compromise of 1877 that led to the withdrawal of federal troops from the South and enabled white supremacist redemption governments. While Reconstruction initially created opportunities for Black political participation, including the election of Black representatives to state legislatures and Congress, these gains were systematically reversed through both legal restrictions and extralegal violence.

Soneta 357: "You are an angry people. Lazy. Dirty. Addicted to incompetence."

This soneta presents racist stereotypes about Black Americans as if spoken by someone with prejudiced views, then responds to these characterizations in the second half. References to "inheritance, opulence—whitelisted by forefathers" expose how systemic advantages have been preserved for white Americans through redlining, restrictive covenants, and other discriminatory practices that built intergenerational wealth for one racial group while systematically excluding others.

Soneta 358: "Judas and the Black Messiah, crucified like a Black pariah,"

Judas and the Black Messiah: 2021 film about Fred Hampton (1948-1969), chairman of the Illinois Black Panther Party, and William O'Neal, the FBI informant who betrayed him. Hampton was only 21 years old when killed by Chicago police in an FBI-coordinated raid. His work established free breakfast programs for children, a community health clinic, educational programs, and political education classes. By late 1969, his Rainbow Coalition brought together Black, Latino, and white working-class organizations across Chicago, threatening FBI Director J. Edgar Hoover's fear of "a messiah who could unify and electrify the militant nationalist movement."

Hoover and his band of hunters: J. Edgar Hoover, FBI Director from 1924-1972, who created the COINTELPRO program targeting civil rights organizations, particularly the Black Panther Party, for surveillance, infiltration, and disruption. FBI tactics included planting false information to create internal conflicts, fabricating evidence to facilitate arrests, and coordinating with local police for raids. Declassified FBI documents revealed that in the Hampton raid, Chicago police fired 99 shots while evidence indicates the Panthers fired only one shot (likely after Hampton had already been killed).

Soneta 359: "You rose upon the ladder we laid"

This is high-tech lynching!: Clarence Thomas's defining defense during his 1991 Supreme Court confirmation hearings, where he portrayed Anita Hill's sexual harassment allegations as a racially motivated attack. He famously declared, "This is a high-tech lynching for uppity Blacks who in any way deign to think for themselves," a calculated rallying cry that helped overshadow Hill's testimony and shift public focus from the allegations to the specter of racial persecution. Ironically, Thomas later rejected race-based protections in his judicial rulings, underscoring the core contradiction this poem seeks to expose.

Thomas with whiteface: This line indicts Clarence Thomas for rising on civil—rights gains and then working to dismantle them. After Thurgood Marshall—the first Black Supreme Court justice—retired, The Los Angeles Times reported that President George H.W. Bush removed white male candidates from consideration, ensuring a Black replacement. Thomas, who had only one year on the D.C. Circuit, was chosen. Although he attended Yale Law under affirmative action—later calling his degree "tainted"—Thomas opposed such policies once on the Court (Students for Fair Admissions v. Harvard, 2023) and voted to weaken other race—conscious protections (Shelby County v. Holder, 2013). By depicting him with "whiteface," this poem argues he exploited race to gain power, including "pulling the race card"—only to burn the deck so another Clarence could never follow.

Soneta 360: "Mtu Mweupe Karibu! White man, you are welcome."

Mtu Mweupe Karibu! White man, you are welcome.: This Swahili phrase (widely spoken in East Africa, particularly Kenya and Tanzania) is employed here with an awareness of its historical and literary weight, including its significant use in David Rubadiri's poem "Stanley Meets Mutesa." In Rubadiri's work, these words are spoken by Kabaka Mutesa I of Buganda to the explorer Henry Morton Stanley, a moment marking the complex and pivotal arrival of Western influence in Africa, as that poem memorably concludes, "And the West is let in." This soneta uses the historically charged welcome to introduce themes of colonial impact and the enduring presence of external cultural dominance.

Trail of Tears: The immediate pivot in the next line to "And so began our Trail of Tears" refers to the forced relocation of Native American nations (primarily Cherokee, Creek,

Chickasaw, Choctaw, and Seminole) from their southeastern homelands to territories west of the Mississippi River between 1830-1850. During these forced marches, an estimated 15,000 indigenous people died from exposure, disease, and starvation. The juxtaposition in this soneta connects the broader implications of such colonial "welcomes" to specific historical atrocities like the Trail of Tears, and further, to the ongoing cultural colonization explored in subsequent lines like "We wear his clothes whenever we work and play— / He ties our hands, so can never close the doors."

Soneta 361: "We can never forget, nor should we ever accept,"

Lumumba: Patrice Lumumba (1925-1961), the first Prime Minister of the independent Democratic Republic of Congo. After advocating for complete Congolese independence from Belgian colonial interests, he was deposed in a coup supported by Belgium and the United States, then executed. President Eisenhower authorized the CIA to eliminate Lumumba, as revealed in the Church Committee investigations of the 1970s and subsequently declassified documents. Belgium officially acknowledged "moral responsibility" for his assassination only in 2002. Lumumba's famous speech at Congo's independence ceremony on June 30, 1960 declared: "We are no longer your monkeys" to the Belgian authorities, asserting African dignity in the face of colonial condescension.

Soneta 364: "Wicked winds did shake the tranquil figs of May,"

It was the worst of times: Echoes the opening line of Charles Dickens' "A Tale of Two Cities" (1859): "It was the best of times, it was the worst of times." The soneta omits "the best of times," presenting an era of unmitigated hardship without counterbalancing hope or progress.

The imagery of "crushing fogs of crime" and "fields filled with mines" creates an apocalyptic landscape where moral corruption has physical manifestations. The final lines describe a total moral collapse where people are "Damned... to hell, turned... to beasts without den," portraying a loss of both spiritual salvation and basic humanity.

Soneta 365: "When hope is gone, god becomes the opium"

Opium of the poor: References Karl Marx's statement that "Religion is the opium of the people" (1843), arguing that religion dulls the pain of oppression while preventing people from addressing its root causes. The soneta applies this to contemporary Lagos, where religious fervor functions as a response to social despair.

The depiction of Lagos residents as "like sheep for slaughter" draws on biblical imagery from Isaiah 53:7 and Psalm 44:22, traditionally interpreted as describing sacrificial suffering. The poem repurposes this imagery to reveal exploitation rather than redemptive sacrifice, with the repeated religious services (listed by days of the week) offering temporary comfort rather than substantive change.

BOOK IV:
THE RETURN

Prophet's Tongue

(Sonetas 366-376)

SONETA 366

To sound like the rush of a billion waves
Crashing wild against the glistening shore;
To mount like the wings of a million cranes
Flapping hard against the roaring pour;
To charge with the weight of a billion bulls
Breaking down the rodeo walls. Glory, friend, isn't for fools.

SONETA 367

I will say it loud. I will not suggest.
Will blare it loud though I walk through the valley
Of the shadow of death, and my soul is depressed:
Beyond Gaza, Darkness sits in Galilee. Sleeps with Zion—intimately.
But I have no fears tonight what scourge I'm gored—
Mine eyes have seen the coming glory of the Lord.

SONETA 368

The justice of heaven weighs too hard to bear,
The moral arc of universe too long, too wide
To tell. Righteous men perish in their righteousness,
Wicked men flourish in their wickedness—without fear.
How I'd wished mercy's rain fell not on every side—
On good, on evil; but shared intimately our hopelessness.

SONETA 369

Everything happens with God in hindsight. No providence an oversight—
No joy too fond, sorrow too stunned, indifference too dense;
When all our foresights and insights are recite and rewrite—
Tablets and scrolls to Him who our story did commence,
Before our eyes could learn to write, our lips pronounce—
The sacred tragedy of being, the joyous melody of Light.

SONETA 370

The Negro dreams of numbers. Integers. Algebra. Wonders what fraction
Of a decimal, raised to the power Color,
Divided by Big Brother, multiplied by poverty, maternal murder,
Equals Justice, Freedom, Equity. He counts, and recounts—Additions. Subtractions.
The Negro dreams of numbers, wonders how in the Badger,
6% Sconnies = 42% bodies living up the river.

SONETA 371

I shall not say to you, *You are my muse,*
For muses do use and abuse drooly pen,—
Cruelly woo with fragrant thoughts and radiant plots,
To later lose like polished stone dull with use.
Hence, I call you dues, which I pay Zeus; Then,
Being due, are the fairest cost of my dearest thoughts.

SONETA 372

Poetry man, bring me your catalog of discontent,
Your registry of grievances, your ledger of maladies.
You howl and you shout to sell a book,
Pretend you care—like suffering is surreal, dire, and urgent.
You hawk your goods like a turbulence of melodies;
But we know, truly, you're one of us—a crook.

SONETA 373

Sing on, poet of sorrow, sadness, and horror—
If the world were not broken, and her rivers bitter,
You'd wail to high heavens, seethe her goodness was dour,
And her flowers sour—her dancing hues a fleeting error.
Were the world the Eden of your visions, would your
Noon shine as nightmare, or your song tenor with splendor?

SONETA 374

We read what we know, abandon what we don't.
How then shall an idea whose time has come,
Whose destiny's to fly—wide, free, and be known,—
Rise above the bars of ignorant men—satisfied but dumb?
My people fall like autumn leaves, wither like hollowed reed,
While knowledge cries in silent texts, yearning to be freed.

SONETA 375

Break forth, break forth! O fertile land of blessed memory;
Hallowed be your harvest—land of rivers, land of timber.
Are these not your children, golden pyramids, tall as giraffes?
Your Kandake of Kush—stopper of Rome and his army?
O blessed land of gold, diamond, cobalt, platinum, coltan, copper—
Rise to shake these grounds—pound like a million staffs!

SONETA 376

You gave it your ALL. And you lost.
But did you? Was it the call you didn't make?
The talk you didn't give? The line you left uncrossed?
Did you lose ALL like house caught in a quake?
Mangled your flesh in the wreck—what should have done,
What could have been. Forgot ALL, your ALL, has won.

Time's Weight

(Sonetas 377-390)

SONETA 377

Glad times, dark times. Bad times, happy times.
Who can foretell the rhyme that keeps the tide
From spilling her banks, drowning my mind with every climb?
The augurs cannot decide which chalice hides their guide,
The falconer cannot divine which way the falcon shall fly.
Good God! What tempest, what jamboree, awaits my flooded eye?

SONETA 378

Past is present, like frayed cloth caught in the wind,
Whipping, weaving—journeying from east to west,
West to east—our lives her wardrobe of archives.
What shall be has been; past and future are twinned.
And what is, was once, for all of man's best,
And worst, are one—constant. Every action revives, and survives.

SONETA 379

We must remember, for the key to the future
Lies buried in the past; the catalog of our dialogues
Hides, like treasure, the picture of our nature.
If past is prologue, then all our days are analogues,
Mirroring us to ourselves—like Groundhog Day: beauty and ashes,
Daffodils and cinders. Those who forget history demand her whiplashes.

SONETA 380

The times taunt me now; like a stone
On sun-soaked shore, awaiting the return of the tide—
Ever so close in memory, never to hold so closely.
The savor of your breath that kindles my bone,
Laughter of the years, coursing my arteries, tickling my side.
The times taunt me now. I hear you. But ghostly.

SONETA 381

Like the throbs of an aging wound that will
Not dull, my heart pounds the walls—a restless drum,
Filling buckets of heart with waters too ill,
Too rough to touch, yet so tender, wishing you'd come.
I've stayed up in the longest night for the light
Of your face, crashing against the wildest waves, without respite.

SONETA 382

This Cold War of words we are in—ticking magma,
Where silence breathes like bombs that never detonate.
Missiles aimed and trained—should they ever rain
Down like meteors on Bourbon Street at Mardi Gras,
The very heart of you and me would obliterate, eviscerate.
This Cold War of words—Mutually Assured Destruction. Mad. Insane.

SONETA 383

If I could have chosen a raiment to wear
Some flimsy garment to cleave to this dateless soul,
Would I the vestment of a carpenter, sewn without seam,
Drape upon my soul? Would a robe of purple bear
Upon this steadfast frame, so legions kneel beneath my sole.
Would a garb of Blackness choose, when Whiteness has esteem.

SONETA 384

I'm sorry I've bothered you with my troubles,
Clobbered you with my endless foibles
Faulted you like you were the riddle to my struggles
Treated you like you've hobbled forever in my shoes—
Hung within your skin the trauma of my bruise.
I'm sorry I thought you knew my Blackness didn't choose.

SONETA 385

Return to slumber, dear brother! The struggle is over.
The waiting is over. At last, the mountaintop we've conquered.
Redline may gash through city blocks like Grim Reaper,
Strangling colored homes, stifling colored growth,—segregated and cornered,
But who's watching, dear brother? Better to rest and sleep
Than stay woke, clowned, and dragged for thinking too deep.

SONETA 386

I've had rainbows in my clouds, swirling all around;
Sunny at times with taunting forecast of thunder
Wintry at times with frigid warning to take cover;
I've had rainbows in my clouds, jumping all around,
Sometimes with sweltering nightmares, and nowhere to shelter,
Sometimes running through my pores, with honeyed aloe, and cucumber.

SONETA 387

God dwells in no house outside of me,
No tower so great, no hall so large that seats
The King of kings, or mighty Lord of lords enthrone.
I've climbed the highest peak, roamed the wildest sea,
Granite walls with marble glitz on gilded stilts,—
Empty rooms, whitewashed tombs—when I'm His living stone.

SONETA 388

A God I must fast to feel, fast to see,
Fast so I'm still, is no God who dwells within,
No God who left His throne, tabernacled with me—
Immanuel, Immanuel—whose coming our mourning has turned to feast.
Yet many who drink the wine from olden wineskin,
Straightaway reject His new. *The old,* they say, *is best.*

SONETA 389

What is the truth? Is it too far to see?
Darkly like the Pharisee, and the Sadducee,
Who sit in Moses' seat, opposed to heresy,
Yet fight to keep what must decay from old decree.
The manna fed awhile, but perfect could not be,
Till Bread of Life appeared. Yet, eat manna over He?

SONETA 390

We spoke before we wrote, so the body truly knows
What truth the soul beholds, long before the cold
Of tight-knit words, hit the nose of brain-lit Thought.
Poetry, more than prose, pours forth as water flows—
Carrying polished stones of old, the truth we hold.
Poetry, then, is rhythm before reason. Gut before plot.

Children of Light

(Sonetas 391-400)

SONETA 391

April is the truest month, the fullest song
From Nature's lungs, springing far and wide with psalmic tongue,
Telling Death and Gloom, winter's hatchet men, devil's tombstone's fallen,
The King's arisen—so Creation rejoice, for Despair is broken.
Bluest skies pour happy tears, wildest lilacs prance everywhere—
Darkness is vanquished, Sadness demolished, when April is here.

SONETA 392

Love is a habit. How can it not be?
Are we not the air we daily breathe,
The grounds we daily walk, sights we daily see?
Then, love is no grand wonder,—no golden wreath
Layered with dazzling stars, fancy wings, and magic friends;
But a quiet sum of countless deeds that never ends.

SONETA 393

Never knew a fish could climb.
Never knew a whale could dive a thousand feet
Hold his breath beneath the silent deep, hours a-time.
Never knew a swift could fly, and sleep, and tweet,
For half the year without perching to rest his arm.
Never knew I could walk on water, quiet the storm.

SONETA 394

I count on God to make it happen
Where my foot has no map, and my eyes
No star to guide where King of Jews was born.
I trust His providence to light my starless wagon,
Bring me to cabin of promised rest. Fire or ice,
Faith's in Him, who gives comfort to those who mourn.

SONETA 395

The night must come for daybreak to form,
Jackals must hunt so the rabbits can run,
Stretch their lungs, test their hinds—know survival through harm.
For *if you have run with footmen*, my dear son,
And are wearied, how shall you contend with horsemen?
If you faint in day of adversity, where's your semen?

SONETA 396

We must not break, nor dare dwell in fear.
Though our feet are pierced, blackburned by the stings
We wear—the fiery serpent and the scorpion, deadly
Armies of a wilderness fierce, thirsty, and bare.
Let's march on—Goshen to Canaan—till our voices ring:
Free at last, free at last! Thank Almighty, we're free!

SONETA 397

Let my body return with me, and keep my spirit
And my soul. What use were they anyways
Whilst they were with me? Were they not always split
Deep within me, knit to your every breath, like rays
Of sunlight, bound to the sun? So then, take what
Was always yours. And leave me what must surely rot.

SONETA 398

I've loved you, not from poverty of palette,
Like a starving artist, barren of means and fine palate;
But I've loved you of necessity where no other colors,
Or flaming hues, rich and decadent, soothe like your flowers.
I've loved you with the darkest and brightest blues
Of every ocean. Shall love you still, if you choose.

SONETA 399

I return to you like a child lost
And in need of love. Not that I've found
A world without its flaws, summer without its frost,
But concussed by a world without your touch, your sound.
If to love were to die a torturous death
Then I've loved you a million times with every breath.

SONETA 400

Is this how it all ends?
Is this how it all begins? My hand in air,
Surrendered to the fear of this long affair.
Never make a deal with the devil, he always pretends,
Momma says, *Always be a daredevil, never give an inch*
To the devil, Poppa says. To flinch or to clinch?

BENEDICTION

Give us the Grace to Brave the Day,
The Faith to not Delay, but Hasten to Save Always—
The Pained and the Lame, the Chained and the Prey.
Help us to Straighten our Ways, Sail this Maze,
For our Traits bait us Astray, take us as Slaves.
To Love Neighbor as Self, Train us—Savior who Saves.

Endnotes for BOOK IV: THE RETURN

Prophet's Tongue (Sonetas 366-376)

Soneta 366: "To sound like the rush of a billion waves"

This opening soneta of Book IV functions as a poetic manifesto, establishing the prophetic voice that characterizes "The Return" section. The repeated structure "To sound like... To mount like... To charge with..." draws from the rhetorical tradition of Hebrew prophetic literature, particularly Isaiah and Jeremiah, where natural imagery conveys divine power. The closing statement that "Glory, friend, isn't for fools" connects to the biblical wisdom tradition (especially Proverbs and Ecclesiastes) where folly and wisdom are contrasted. The poem positions authentic poetic expression as requiring both courage and wisdom.

Soneta 367: "I will say it loud. I will not suggest."

The valley of the shadow of death: References Psalm 23:4, "Yea, though I walk through the valley of the shadow of death, I will fear no evil." The biblical psalm's message of faith amid dire circumstances is recontextualized for contemporary struggles, particularly regarding Gaza as mentioned in the poem.

Mine eyes have seen the coming glory of the Lord: Quotes the opening line of Julia Ward Howe's "The Battle Hymn of the Republic" (1861). Written during the Civil War, the song frames the Union cause as divinely sanctioned, connecting military victory to divine judgment. The soneta invokes this language of prophetic witness in a new context of resistance to injustice. This connection to abolitionist tradition positions contemporary moral witness within a historical lineage of prophetic speaking against oppression.

Soneta 368: "The justice of heaven weighs too hard to bear,"

The moral arc of universe: References Martin Luther King Jr.'s frequent statement that "The arc of the moral universe is long, but it begins toward justice." King adapted this from 19th-century Unitarian minister Theodore Parker's sermon. King's use of this phrase reflected his theological understanding of divine justice working through history, even when immediate evidence suggested otherwise. As a Baptist minister, King grounded his civil rights work in a prophetic tradition that understood God as ultimately vindicating the oppressed, a perspective that sustained hope during setbacks and violence.

The soneta examines the tension between this hopeful vision and the immediate reality of suffering, challenging the patience such a view requires from those experiencing injustice firsthand. The closing lines—"How I'd wished mercy's rain fell not on every side— / On good, on evil; but shared intimately our hopelessness"—confront the theological problem of why divine justice allows evil to prosper and the righteous to suffer, a theme central to the biblical book of Job.

Soneta 369: "Everything happens with God in hindsight. No providence an oversight—"

This soneta explores divine providence—the theological concept that God directs all events toward ultimate purpose. The poem frames human experiences, both joyful and sorrowful, as "tablets and scrolls to Him who our story did commence," positioning human history within a divine narrative. The final lines describe existence as both "sacred tragedy" and "joyous melody," capturing the dual nature of life as containing both suffering and beauty under divine oversight. This theological perspective draws from Augustine's concept of evil as privation rather than substance—part of God's permissive rather than active will.

Soneta 370: "The Negro dreams of numbers. Integers. Algebra."

Badger: Refers to Wisconsin, nicknamed the "Badger State."

6% Sconnies = 42% bodies living up the river: Addresses racial disparities in Wisconsin's criminal justice system. African Americans comprise approximately 6% of Wisconsin's population ("Sconnies" is slang for Wisconsin residents) but constitute about 42% of the state's prison population. "Up the river" is colloquial for imprisonment, originally referring to Sing Sing prison located up the Hudson River from New York City.

The mathematical language throughout the poem transforms abstract statistical disparities into existential questions, personifying "the Negro" as seeking a mathematical formula that could explain or resolve structural inequalities. The repeated references to mathematical operations ("Additions. Subtractions") portray the exhausting mental calculations required to navigate systems designed with embedded racial disparities.

Soneta 371: "I shall not say to you, You are my muse,"

This soneta rejects the classical concept of the muse—the divine source of artistic inspiration in Greek mythology. Instead of depicting inspiration as external and fickle ("muses do use and abuse drooly pen,— / Cruelly woo with fragrant thoughts and radiant plots"), the poem reframes the creative relationship as economic: "I call you dues, which I pay Zeus." This transforms inspiration from gift to transaction, from passive reception to active commitment. The final line, "Being due, are the fairest cost of my dearest thoughts," suggests that authentic creation requires payment rather than merely awaiting visitation from the muse.

Soneta 372: "Poetry man, bring me your catalog of discontent,"

This soneta challenges the authenticity of poetic protest, questioning whether poets who "howl and... shout to sell a book" genuinely care about the suffering they describe or merely commodify it. The accusation that poets "Pretend you care—like suffering is surreal, dire, and urgent" critiques the potential exploitation inherent in transforming others' pain into marketable art. The final line's twist—"But we know, truly, you're one of us—a crook"—implicates both poet and reader in this system of aesthetic consumption, suggesting complicity rather than moral superiority.

Soneta 373: "Sing on, poet of sorrow, sadness, and horror—"

This soneta extends the critique from Soneta 372, examining how poets are drawn to darkness and suffering rather than celebration. The hypothetical—"If the world were not broken, and her rivers bitter, / You'd wail to high heavens, seethe her goodness was dour"—challenges the poetic preference for lamentation over praise. This critique connects to the classical dispute between poetry of witness (testifying to suffering) and poetry of beauty (celebrating goodness), questioning whether poetic vision is inherently attracted to darkness or whether this focus constitutes an ethical response to a genuinely broken world.

Soneta 375: "Break forth, break forth! O fertile land of blessed memory;"

Kandake of Kush stopper of Rome and his army: References Queen Amanirenas, a Kandake (queen) of the ancient Nubian kingdom of Kush who successfully fought against Roman expansion around 24 BCE. After Roman forces under Governor Petronius invaded Kushite territory and captured the city of Napata, Amanirenas led a counterattack that ultimately resulted in a peace treaty favorable to Kush. Archaeological evidence includes a bronze head of Emperor Augustus discovered buried beneath temple steps in Meroe, likely taken during her forces' raids.

Land of gold, diamond, cobalt, platinum, coltan, copper: Lists valuable natural resources abundant in Africa. Coltan, particularly, is essential for modern electronics manufacturing (used in smartphones and computers) and has been linked to conflict mining in the Democratic Republic of Congo, where its extraction has funded armed groups and perpetuated violence.

The prophetic command to "Rise to shake these grounds—pound like a million staffs!" connects to Moses's staff that performed miracles in Egypt (Exodus 7-10). This biblical allusion envisions Africa reclaiming its resources and heritage with divine—like authority, transforming from exploited land to empowered actor on the world stage.

Time's Weight (Sonetas 377-390)

Soneta 377: "Glad times, dark times. Bad times, happy times."

The reference to "the falconer cannot divine which way the falcon shall fly" echoes W.B. Yeats' "The Second Coming" (1919): "The falcon cannot hear the falconer." Where Yeats used this image to signify societal collapse and loss of order, this soneta applies it to personal uncertainty.

Soneta 378: "Past is present, like frayed cloth caught in the wind,"

What shall be has been; past and future are twinned: Echoes Ecclesiastes 1:9, "What has been will be again, what has been done will be done again; there is nothing new under the sun." This biblical view of cyclical history appears as both philosophical insight and warning.

Soneta 379: "We must remember, for the key to the future"

Past is prologue: Quotes from Shakespeare's "The Tempest" (Act 2, Scene 1): "What's past is prologue." Originally suggesting that past events set the stage for murder, the phrase has evolved to mean that history provides context for the present. The soneta uses this to declare that historical memory is essential for understanding contemporary events.

Groundhog Day: References the 1993 film in which the protagonist relives the same day repeatedly. The soneta uses this popular culture reference to illustrate the cyclical nature of history—beauty and destruction, progress and regression continually repeating. The phrase "Those who forget history summon her whiplashes" updates George Santayana's famous observation that "Those who cannot remember the past are condemned to repeat it," adding the dimension of punishment for historical amnesia.

Soneta 382: "This Cold War of words we are in—ticking magma,"

Cold War: Period of geopolitical tension between the United States and Soviet Union from 1947-1991, characterized by political maneuvering, propaganda, and proxy conflicts rather than direct military engagement between the superpowers.

Mutually Assured Destruction: Nuclear deterrence doctrine stating that full-scale use of nuclear weapons by opposing sides would cause the complete annihilation of both attacker and defender. Often abbreviated as MAD, it exemplified the potential for total destruction underlying superficial peace. The soneta applies this concept to interpersonal conflict, transforming nuclear strategy into relationship metaphor. The "silence [that] breathes like bombs that never detonate" depicts unspoken tensions as explosive devices that maintain destructive potential even when dormant.

Soneta 383: "If I could have chosen a raiment to wear"

This soneta explores identity as clothing—a "raiment" or "vestment" one might choose rather than inherit. The options presented span biblical and historical references: "vestment of a carpenter, sewn without seam" alludes to Christ's garment in John 19:23; "robe of purple" indicates royalty; "queen of ancient Kush" references the African kingdom discussed in Soneta 374. The final question—"Would a garb of Blackness choose, when Whiteness has esteem"—directly confronts racial hierarchy, positioning race as a "garment" whose social value is artificially determined.

Soneta 384: "I'm sorry I've bothered you with my troubles,"

This soneta addresses white fatigue with racial discourse, apologizing ironically for "clobbered you with my endless foibles" and "Faulted you like you were the riddle to my struggles." The repeated structure of "I'm sorry" builds through increasingly pointed observations until the final revelation: "I'm sorry I thought you knew my Blackness didn't choose." This closing line connects to Soneta 383's examination of identity as clothing, but inverts it—declaring that racial identity, unlike a chosen garment, is not voluntarily adopted. The poem simultaneously acknowledges white exhaustion with racial discussions while refusing to accept this as justification for disengagement.

Soneta 385: "Go back to sleep, dear brother! The struggle is over."

Woke: Term originating in African American Vernacular English signifying awareness of social and racial justice issues. By 2025, the term had undergone significant semantic evolution—embraced by progressive movements as representing necessary consciousness of systemic injustice while simultaneously weaponized by opponents as representing excessive focus on identity politics. The soneta employs irony to critique premature declarations of racial progress, instructing listeners to "rest and sleep / Than stay woke, clowned, and dragged for digging too deep."

Redline may gash through city blocks: References redlining, the discriminatory practice of denying services (particularly financial services like mortgages) to residents of certain areas based on their racial or ethnic composition. The Federal Housing Administration institutionalized this practice in the 1930s by creating color-coded maps marking minority neighborhoods as high-risk, effectively preventing residents from obtaining loans. Though officially banned by the Fair Housing Act of 1968, the practice's effects continue to shape American residential segregation and racial wealth disparities.

Soneta 386: "I've had rainbows in my clouds, swirling all around;"

Rainbows in my clouds: References Maya Angelou's frequent statement: "God put the rainbow in the clouds, not just in the sky, so that each one of us in the dreariest and most dreaded moments can see a possibility of hope." Angelou developed this as a personal philosophy emphasizing finding hope in difficult circumstances.

The soneta expands Angelou's metaphor, detailing the varied "weather" of a life containing both joy and hardship. The repeated phrase "I've had rainbows in my clouds" affirms that hope persists even through changing circumstances. The closing images of "sweltering nightmares" contrasted with "honeyed aloe, and cucumber" capture the oscillation between suffering and comfort that characterizes human experience.

Soneta 387: "God dwells in no house outside of me,"

His living stone: References 1 Peter 2:5, which describes believers as "living stones... built into a spiritual house." The biblical passage reframes temple worship from physical buildings to the community of believers. The soneta extends this metaphor to the individual, declaring "I'm His living stone" after cataloging various impressive structures ("Granite walls with marble glitz on gilded stilts").

This theological perspective draws from Christian tradition that emphasize divine indwelling rather than external temples. The progression from seeking God in magnificent buildings to recognizing divine presence within transforms religious understanding from institutional to personal, from external architecture to internal experience.

Soneta 388: "A God I must fast to feel, fast to see,"

Fast to feel, fast to see: Explores fasting as spiritual discipline in various religious traditions, where abstaining from food aims to heighten spiritual awareness and divine connection. The soneta contrasts this effortful approach to divine presence with a theology of incarnation—"No God who left His throne, tabernacled with me— / Immanuel, Immanuel"—referencing the Christian doctrine that God became human in Jesus Christ (Matthew 1:23: "Immanuel, which means 'God with us'").

The old, they say, is best: References Luke 5:39, "And no one, having drunk old wine, immediately desires new; for he says, 'The old is better.'" Jesus used this metaphor to explain why established religious traditions, particularly the old practice of fasting, resist new teachings.

Soneta 389: "What is the truth? Is it too far to see?"

Pharisee, and the Sadducee: Jewish religious groups during the Second Temple period (approximately 515 BCE to 70 CE). The Pharisees emphasized oral tradition and scriptural interpretation, while the Sadducees were more conservative, accepting only written Torah. Both groups appear in the New Testament, often depicted as opposing Jesus's ministry.

The manna fed awhile: References Exodus 16, where God provided manna (miraculous food) to sustain the Israelites in the wilderness. The soneta contrasts this temporary provision with "Bread of Life," a title Jesus claimed in John 6:35, suggesting progressive revelation where earlier religious understandings give way to fuller ones. The final line—"Till Bread of Life appeared. Yet, eat manna over He?"—presents religious conservatism as choosing familiar but less substantial spiritual nourishment over new revelation.

Children of Light (Sonetas 391-400)

Soneta 391: "April is the truest month, the fullest song"

April is the truest month: Deliberately inverts the famous opening line of T.S. Eliot's "The Waste Land" (1922): "April is the cruellest month." Where Eliot portrayed spring's renewal as painful for a spiritually dead society, this soneta reclaims April as a time of genuine rebirth and resurrection.

The imagery of "Bluest skies pour happy tears, wildest lilacs prance everywhere" creates a scene of natural celebration, contrasting sharply with Eliot's wasteland. The declaration that

"Darkness is vanquished, Sadness demolished, when April is here" positions seasonal renewal as spiritual victory, connecting physical spring to emotional and spiritual rebirth. This places the poem within the tradition of resurrection symbolism that spans religious and literary traditions.

Soneta 392: "Love is a habit. How can it not be?"

This soneta redefines love from romantic ideal to daily practice—"Love is a habit." By connecting love to routine actions rather than overwhelming emotion, the poem challenges the conception of love as "grand wonder,—no golden wreath / Layered with dazzling stars, fancy wings, and magic friends." Instead, it defines love as "a quiet sum of countless deeds that never ends," grounding transcendent feeling in concrete action.

This perspective connects to philosophical traditions from Aristotle to contemporary virtue ethics that emphasize character formation through habitual practice rather than momentary inspiration. By positioning love as "the air we daily breathe, / The grounds we daily walk," the poem places it within the realm of the ordinary rather than the exceptional.

Soneta 393: "Never knew a fish could climb."

Walk on water, quiet the storm: References two of Jesus's miracles described in the Gospels: walking on the Sea of Galilee (Matthew 14:22-33) and calming a storm that threatened his disciples' boat (Mark 4:35-41). The soneta places these supernatural acts alongside natural wonders of animal adaptation, connecting divine and natural capabilities that exceed human limitations. The repeated structure "Never knew" creates a catalog of surprising capabilities, culminating in the human ability to "walk on water, quiet the storm." This progression from animal abilities (fish climbing, whales diving, birds sleeping while flying) to human spiritual capacity suggests a continuity between natural and supernatural phenomena as manifestations of unexpected possibility.

Notable examples include the Mangrove Killifish (Kryptolebias marmoratus), which can live out of water for extended periods and climb tree roots; the Cuvier's beaked whale (Ziphius cavirostris), which holds records for diving nearly 3,000 meters and for breath-hold duration (one exceeding 3.5 hours); and the Alpine swift (Tachymarptis melba), which can remain in continuous flight for over six months, likely engaging in unihemispheric sleep.

Soneta 395: "The night must come for daybreak to form,"

If you have run with footmen... contend with horsemen: Quotes Jeremiah 12:5, "If you have run with footmen and they have wearied you, then how can you contend with horses?" The biblical passage establishes that current trials prepare one for greater challenges.

If you faint in day of adversity, where's your semen?: References Proverbs 24:10, "If you faint in the day of adversity, your strength is small." The soneta recasts "strength" as "semen," linking spiritual resilience to generative potential.

The opening lines—"The night must come for daybreak to form, / Jackals must hunt so the rabbits can run"—establish adversity as necessary for development. This perspective frames challenges not as obstacles to overcome but as essential components of strength-building, connecting physical evolution ("Stretch their lungs, test their hinds") to spiritual growth.

Soneta 396: "We cannot despair. We must not give room to fear."

Goshen to Canaan: References the biblical Exodus journey. Goshen was the region in Egypt where the Israelites lived before the Exodus; Canaan was the Promised Land they sought. This journey through the wilderness became a central metaphor in liberation theology and African American spiritual tradition, symbolizing the path from oppression to freedom.

Free at last, free at last! Thank Almighty, we're free!: Echoes the conclusion of Martin Luther King Jr.'s "I Have a Dream" speech (1963): "Free at last! Free at last! Thank God Almighty, we are free at last!" King himself was quoting an old spiritual, demonstrating how liberation language passes through generations of Black resistance.

The biblical imagery of "the fiery serpent and the scorpion" from Deuteronomy 8:15 describes the dangers of wilderness journey, while the command to "march on" despite these perils connects individual perseverance to collective progress. The poem links personal spiritual journey to historical liberation movements, positioning individual courage within communal struggle.

Soneta 400: "Is this how it all ends?"

This concluding soneta of the collection addresses the moment of capitulation—"My hand in air, / Surrendered to the fear of this long affair." The competing parental voices—"Never make a deal with the devil, he always pretends, / Momma says, Always be a daredevil, never give an inch / To the devil, Poppa says"—present contradictory moral guidance about resistance versus accommodation.

The final question—"To flinch or to clinch?"—deliberately echoes Shakespeare's "To be or not to be" from Hamlet's famous soliloquy. Both present existential dilemmas as binary choices at moments of moral crisis. Where Hamlet contemplates suicide versus continued suffering, the speaker here faces the choice between resistance (clinch) or yielding (flinch). This open conclusion transforms the book from statement to question, from closed discourse to ongoing conversation. As the final poem before the benediction, it acknowledges that moral struggle continues even after prophetic revelation, historical understanding, and spiritual insight have been achieved.

About the Poet

Pelumi Olatinpo is a poet, a philosopher, a pioneer, a prophet of possibility, and a provocateur of our collective consciousness. Author of *Poeta: Sonetas and Sonnets*, where he introduced the innovative soneta form, he is also a DREAMer and technical startup founder who sees our world for what it can be, not just what it is. An American-Nigerian, he lives with his wife and two kids in the Washington, D.C., area, where he serves on the Montgomery County Commission on Homelessness.

"I do not come to you alone. Naked. Without guests."

JOIN THE WITNESS

MANIFEST DESTINY exists not only as a volume of witness, but as part of an ongoing dialogue about our shared human experience.

For those who wish to remain connected:

The Poet

Instagram: @pelumiolatinpo
X (formerly Twitter): @pelumiolatinpo

TogetherInWitness

We publish socio-conscious literary works that console, celebrate, and challenge our collective consciousness.

Our mission is to amplify diverse voices and stories that inspire thought and drive positive change.

We believe in the power of literature to shape society—not only by witnessing what is, but by imagining what could be.

Website: www.TogetherInWitness.org
Instagram: @togetherinwitness
Email: hello@togetherinwitness.org